Number 108
Winter 2005

New Directions for Evaluation

Jean A. King
Editor-in-Chief

# Evaluating Nonformal Education Programs and Settings

Emma Norland
Cindy Somers
Editors

EVALUATING NONFORMAL EDUCATION PROGRAMS AND SETTINGS
*Emma Norland, Cindy Somers* (eds.)
New Directions for Evaluation, no. 108
*Jean A. King,* Editor-in-Chief

Microfilm copies of issues and articles are available in 16mm and 35mm, as well as microfiche in 105mm, through University Microfilms Inc., 300 North Zeeb Road, Ann Arbor, Michigan 48106-1346.

*New Directions for Evaluation* is indexed in Contents Pages in Education, Higher Education Abstracts, and Sociological Abstracts.

NEW DIRECTIONS FOR EVALUATION (ISSN 1097-6736, electronic ISSN 1534-875X) is part of The Jossey-Bass Education Series and is published quarterly by Wiley Subscription Services, Inc., a Wiley company, at Jossey-Bass, 989 Market Street, San Francisco, California 94103-1741.

SUBSCRIPTIONS cost $80.00 for U.S./Canada/Mexico; $104 international. For institutions, agencies, and libraries, $185 U.S.; $225 Canada; $259 international. Prices subject to change.

EDITORIAL CORRESPONDENCE should be addressed to the Editor-in-Chief, Jean A. King, University of Minnesota, 330 Wulling Hall, 86 Pleasant Street SE, Minneapolis, MN 55455.

www.josseybass.com

# Editorial Policy and Procedures

*New Directions for Evaluation,* a quarterly sourcebook, is an official publication of the American Evaluation Association. The journal publishes empirical, methodological, and theoretical works on all aspects of evaluation. A reflective approach to evaluation is an essential strand to be woven through every volume. The editors encourage volumes that have one of three foci: (1) craft volumes that present approaches, methods, or techniques that can be applied in evaluation practice, such as the use of templates, case studies, or survey research; (2) professional issue volumes that present issues of import for the field of evaluation, such as utilization of evaluation or locus of evaluation capacity; (3) societal issue volumes that draw out the implications of intellectual, social, or cultural developments for the field of evaluation, such as the women's movement, communitarianism, or multiculturalism. A wide range of substantive domains is appropriate for *New Directions for Evaluation;* however, the domains must be of interest to a large audience within the field of evaluation. We encourage a diversity of perspectives and experiences within each volume, as well as creative bridges between evaluation and other sectors of our collective lives.

The editors do not consider or publish unsolicited single manuscripts. Each issue of the journal is devoted to a single topic, with contributions solicited, organized, reviewed, and edited by a guest editor. Issues may take any of several forms, such as a series of related chapters, a debate, or a long article followed by brief critical commentaries. In all cases, the proposals must follow a specific format, which can be obtained from the editor-in-chief. These proposals are sent to members of the editorial board and to relevant substantive experts for peer review. The process may result in acceptance, a recommendation to revise and resubmit, or rejection. However, the editors are committed to working constructively with potential guest editors to help them develop acceptable proposals.

Jean A. King, Editor-in-Chief
University of Minnesota
330 Wulling Hall
86 Pleasant Street SE
Minneapolis, MN 55455
e-mail: kingx004@umn.edu

# CONTENTS

# Editors' Notes

Billions of dollars are spent annually on nonformal, informal, and nontraditional education programs and collaborative formal and nonformal efforts. Public and private dollars fund literally thousands of programs, and yet the field of program evaluation to date has provided little guidance for evaluating such efforts. There are precious few resources available to lead program administrators, staff, and evaluators through the maze of programs and the diversity of the constituencies that support them. The stakeholders and audiences of nonformal education programs are numerous: literacy advocates; Boy Scout parents; extension education families; National Park volunteers; Elder Hostel participants; watershed science groups; HIV/AIDS patients' caregivers; visitors to archeological, art, and children's museums; historical monument restoration advocates; teachers in schools using the environment as an integrating context; and many others. These programs can range from a one-shot, hour-long lecture to an ongoing, one-day-a-week volunteer program, to a three-week study tour, to a four-weekends-across-one-year work camp, to a "stop by when you can" museum collection.

This volume explores the issues that evaluators of nonformal education programs and settings (such as parks, zoos, community outreach organizations, and museums) struggle with. These issues are not so much unique to nonformal programs and settings, but rather pose different sets of problems and solutions from those associated with traditional education programs. The chapter authors address this topic from extensive experience as both evaluators and education professionals who have worked in nonformal education settings. The group includes independent evaluation consultants and internal evaluators as well as university professors, doctoral students, program directors, and other program staff.

To develop the content for the volume and to gather stories from different settings, we participated in a planning retreat in June 2004 at the Great Smoky Mountains Institute at Tremont in Townsend, Tennessee. It was a novel idea to use an authors' retreat to create the content of the volume inductively. For those of us who are nonformal educators or work with them, it made perfect sense to use a nonformal education setting and methods for this task. Not in recent history, if ever, has a group of professional

The editors would like to thank Julia Washburn and the National Park Foundation for funding the authors' retreat that facilitated the planning of this volume.

NEW DIRECTIONS FOR EVALUATION, no. 108, Winter 2005   © Wiley Periodicals, Inc.
Published online in Wiley InterScience (www.interscience.wiley.com) • DOI: 10.1002/ev.166

evaluators whose expertise is the evaluation of nonformal education programs been together to think critically about evaluation issues and share
thoughts and experiences regarding their work. The synergy was amazing.
At the retreat, we started with this task:

> Share a memorable story about an evaluation you did, had done to you, par-
> ticipated in, were a part of, or otherwise know about first hand. . . . Then
> answer some questions about the evaluation: What was the situation? What
> was your role? What happened? What were the biggest evaluation challenges
> or issues? What methods, practices and/or tools were employed to address
> these challenges or issues? What worked well and why? What didn't work so
> well and why? What makes this story memorable? What advice would you
> offer to others doing an evaluation in this situation? What's different or
> unique about doing evaluations in nonformal, informal and other non-
> traditional education programs and settings relative to other arenas?

The stories were both humorous and thought provoking. The participants told tales that vacillated between moments of clear frustration and
bouts of uncontrolled laughter. We recounted unbelievable amounts of detail
and historical and hysterical facts. And all the stories, no matter what they
were about, no matter where they took place, and no matter what role each
of us had played, sounded similar. One thread running through all the stories was the connection of the values of the evaluand (the nonformal education program and those associated with it) with those of the evaluator.

We share this short description because it illustrates the power of the
process we used to generate the ideas for this volume. Publications and individual experiences are important, and we all have them, but the ability to
gather together as experienced evaluators, many of us with program experience as well, and spend what was sometimes similar to hours of intense
focus group interviewing was an amazing experience. It was research, to a
certain extent, and we believe new knowledge was generated that is
included in this volume's content.

Chapter One, by Emma Norland, explores the "nuances of being 'non,'"
defining terms and identifying characteristics of nonformal education programs that necessarily affect their evaluations. In Chapter Two, Kate Wiltz
discusses the multiple roles of an evaluator in nonformal education program
evaluation, highlighting the potential for expanded involvement and relationship building. In Chapter Three, Cindy Somers provides an example of
a participatory evaluation of Denver's Wonders In Nature–Wonders In Neighborhoods Conservation Education Program, detailing the evaluation process
from inception through pilot testing and beyond. Evaluation use in nonformal education settings is the topic of Chapter Four, in which Kate Clavijo
and her coauthors provide suggestions for nonformal education program
decision makers to make use of their investment in evaluation. Chapter Five

tackles two key topics in framing the evaluations of nonformal education programs—the development of program theory and evaluation capacity building. Martha Monroe and her coauthors provide specific ways to attend to both. Chapter Six, by Laurene Christensen, Julie Nielsen, Christopher Rogers, and Boris Volkov, begins to identify the methodological challenges of evaluating nonformal education programs and describes four specific methods to overcome them. The final chapter contains a brief interview by Ruth Bowman and Kelli Johnson with David Smith, a long-time participant on the nonformal education scene, in which he provides his thoughts and evaluation concerns.

The issues related to evaluating nonformal education programs are not new. In fact, we were surprised to see that there was not an earlier *New Directions for Evaluation* volume on this topic or on the topic of extension education evaluation, which is one the largest providers of nonformal education. This volume is surely timely: it addresses an evaluation area that has been largely bypassed in the formal evaluation literature. It is not, however, a how-to book for nonevaluators, new evaluators, or program staff. It is instead meant to illustrate evaluation issues common to nonformal educational programs and settings and to provide ideas for addressing them and new ways of thinking about them. We hope it will raise evaluators' awareness and increase discussion of issues related to evaluation in nonformal education.

Emma Norland
Cindy Somers
Editors

*EMMA NORLAND is consulting social scientist for the Office of Research and Development at the U.S. Environmental Protection Agency and adjunct professor at the American University School of Public Affairs in the Department of Public Administration.*

*CINDY SOMERS is an evaluation and program development consultant working in Denver, Colorado.*

1

*Evaluation in nonformal education programs and settings must be framed within its special context—one that demands elasticity, transformation, and collaboration on the part of evaluators.*

# The Nuances of Being "Non": Evaluating Nonformal Education Programs and Settings

*Emma Norland*

The importance of using evaluation has been heartily argued and widely accepted as all but routine in the traditional, formal education domain. There is less evidence, however, of that recognition and acceptance in nonformal education programs and settings. Understanding the significance and consequence of conducting evaluation as a regular part of program development and implementation is less clear the more the educational program deviates from a traditional structure, context, provider, or setting. Even when evaluation *is* embraced by nonformal education program staff, there tends to be little organizational capacity for conducting evaluation and, many times, only low to mediocre encouragement and support from organizational leadership.

Obviously the extent to which nonformal education programs incorporate evaluation practices and use results varies greatly and tends to be situational rather than systemic. This is both good news and bad news for evaluation advocates. The good news is that, given funding, evaluation can be introduced easily and quickly by hiring a program staff member with evaluation interest or expertise. The bad news is that when that staff member leaves the program or organization, the impetus to continue with evaluation may be lost just as quickly.

This *New Directions* volume examines the nuances of conducting evaluation in nonformal education programs and settings. We examine a set of

NEW DIRECTIONS FOR EVALUATION, no. 108, Winter 2005  © Wiley Periodicals, Inc.
Published online in Wiley InterScience (www.interscience.wiley.com) • DOI: 10.1002/ev.167

universal evaluation issues—evaluator role, stakeholder involvement, program theory, capacity building, strategy selection, and evaluation use—as they occur and interact within nonformal education situations. The examples we have used do not include all the possible purposes, organizations, content, settings, and audiences found across the nonformal education spectrum, but they do share common characteristics. Illustrations come from conservation education; extension education; and education by zoos, aquariums, museums, parks, and community organizations. Our hope is that by presenting snippets from the nonformal education program evaluation world, readers will gain a deeper understanding of the ways in which common evaluation issues manifest themselves in some less common situations.

## Defining Nonformal Education: The Troubling Case of a "Non"

Defining certain words, especially words beginning with the prefix *non*, is best left to dictionaries. Many words beginning with *non* present a somewhat unflattering, even disagreeable picture: *noncommunicative, nonproductive, nonresponsive. Non* suggests the absence of the named characteristic and therefore the opposite of it. Someone who is called *nonproductive* is *not* productive—possessing no productivity. Even when the original word is perceived as negative, such as *judgmental* or *trivial,* and being nonjudgmental or nontrivial would most likely be seen as positive, the original word still serves as the basis for defining the new characteristic and thus the absence of or opposite of that characteristic. So we really do not know exactly what the new characteristic is; we only know what it is not.

So it is with the word *nonformal* when used to describe education. Nonformal education resembles something other than traditional, formal education, but what? Nonformal education is *not formal* education, but what *is* it? Is it the opposite? Is it the absence of formal? As a visual learner, I much prefer drawings and photos over words. And if words must prevail, stories are useful as illustrations and clarifiers. It is with this in mind that we have sprinkled stories from the field throughout this *New Directions* volume to portray more clearly the nature of nonformal education and the experience of evaluating it. However, to set the stage, I have provided a few definitions to consider and some characteristics that many nonformal education programs share.

Before delving into a fuller discussion of *nonformal,* many readers may question the absence of the term *informal education.* While some scholars prefer a distinction between informal and nonformal, we have chosen to use *nonformal* for simplicity to represent all education occurring outside formal classrooms. Even as different definitions were initially created for *informal* and *nonformal* (for an example of a historical perspective, see Rogers, 2004), the distinctions were and still are mostly administrative

(Coombs and Ahmed, 1974). (For excellent discussions regarding informal and nonformal education with an international perspective, review the *Encyclopedia of Informal Education* [Smith, 2005].)

## Defining Characteristics of Nonformal Education

Perhaps the best way to understand nonformal education and its defining characteristics is to examine the similarities among several distinctly different examples.

**Examples.** The Corporation for Public Broadcasting (2002) portrays its concept of nonformal education as that which occurs outside the classroom (after-school programs, community-based organizations, museums, libraries, at home, and so on) and lists these key attributes to distinguish nonformal education: attendance and leadership is inconsistent; learning opportunities are discreet and time-bound; "teachers" vary in abilities, backgrounds, and command of teaching techniques, content expertise, and group management; and multiple sets of standards or lack of any standards allow curriculum flexibility.

Adult basic and literacy education organizations characterize nonformal education as bottom-up education because participation in these types of programs is usually voluntary and necessitates learner involvement at most stages of program conceptualization and implementation. The following elements define a bottom-up adult education program: having a short-term and specific purpose; being noncredential based; being short, recurrent, or part-time occurrences; offering individualized and practical content; using environment-based, community-related, flexible, learner-centered, and resource-saving delivery modes; and controlled by a democratic, learner-dominated process (Fordham, 1993).

A third example is from the out-of-school youth education programs such as 4-H and scouting that are targeted at youth but spend a great deal of resources on nonformal education for adult volunteers working with their education programs. For example, in his 4H youth development *Toolkit for Volunteer Leaders* (2003), Etling offers the characteristics in Table 1.1 contrasting formal and nonformal education programs.

Finally, programs for all ages linked to parks, zoos, and other conservation and environmental organizations provide a fourth distinct example. In their review of the environmental education literature, Marcinkowski and Washburn (personal interview, 2005) suggest five characteristics that help define nonformal environmental education programs:

1. Purposes of nonformal programs are often neither uniformly nor solely educational. Nonformal institutions may embed educational purposes and experiences within a variety of programs that are social and recreational in nature, such as in programs for family groups (Tilden, 1957; Sharpe,

### Table 1.1. Characteristics of Formal and Nonformal Education Programs

| Dimension of Education | Formal | Nonformal |
|---|---|---|
| Focus | Emphasis on teaching | Emphasis on learning |
| Curriculum | Sequential prescribed curriculum | Options, variety, flexibility; often determined by learners |
| Relationships | Teacher–student; often hierarchical | Facilitator–learner informal relationships |
| Resources | Often originate at the state and federal levels. High costs typically associated with formal education | Often local. Low costs are typically associated with nonformal education |
| Time orientation | Future | Immediate |
| Structure | High structure typically required | Low structure often desirable |

*Sources:* Etling (1994), Kahn (1989), and Meredith, Fortner, and Mullins (1997). Thanks to Julie Nielsen for her compilation of this description.

1976; Knapp, 1997; Civitarese, Legg, and Zuefle, 1998; Marcinkowski, 1999; Ham, 1992).

2. Target audiences in nonformal settings include school classes, other groups, and walk-in visitors. First-time classes, groups, and visitors are rarely well known. Furthermore, it can be difficult to describe or characterize visiting groups and walk-in visitors in ways that will guide program development. However, visitor characteristics can be discerned and addressed as part of program delivery, as is commonly done in guided forms of interpretation (Tilden, 1957; Sharpe, 1976; Ham, 1992).

3. Program development in nonformal settings becomes, often by necessity, a decentralized process. The task of program design and development or selection and adaptation often falls to that institution's education staff (Childress, 1976; Disinger, 1981).

4. One of the major concerns of nonformal program and evaluation personnel has been with participant and visitor satisfaction (for example, with the program, instructors, facilities, and support services). This is particularly true for nonformal programs that are dependent on repeat participation or visitation for program revenue or program justification (Chenery and Hammerman, 1984–1985).

5. Participant exposure to programs in nonformal settings varies widely, ranging from a visit of an hour or two, to a full day, to several days. Furthermore, when there is an opportunity for extended program exposure (for example, classes or groups for youth), this is more likely to occur on an intermittent basis (for example, after-school and weekend clubs) than on a continuous basis (as in schools).

**Themes Across the Examples.**  Three themes are present across these examples of nonformal education programs: elasticity, transformation, and collaborative adventure.

*Elasticity.*  Nonformal education programs and processes anticipate and welcome diversity and the invariable changes that occur in all elements of the teaching-learning exchange. They make room for originality and accommodate differences by using adaptation, tolerance, and flexibility. An obvious implication of this elasticity of nonformal education is that common practices do not necessarily apply. For example, in the world of formal education, a percentage of the budget is sometimes set aside for a program's evaluation. This is generally not the case in nonformal education, as I learned years ago. When I shared the percentage rule with the head of a struggling nonprofit organization looking for evaluation support for his educational programs, he quickly explained that "a percent of nothin' is still nothing."

The reality for many nonformal education organizations is that they are implementing low-budget programs and lower-budget evaluations. A recent experience highlights one way in which evaluators can assist nonformal educators in stretching the boundaries of budgets by using some unusual cost-saving strategies:

> I stayed at the home of a member of the science center's board of directors for a week to conduct a scoping visit. This arrangement was reached through the pleading of the science center's director of education, the gracious hospitality of the board member, and my knowledge that if I did not agree to cost-cutting measures such as sleeping in a strange home, the possibility of any evaluation work at the science center would be nil.

Evaluation on a nonformal shoestring may require evaluators to analyze focus group data without transcriptions, rely on program staff to enter survey data, or use youth participants to collect systematic observation data on the museum floor.

*Transformation.*  All individuals involved in nonformal education, including learners, teachers, administrators, and stakeholders, can experience benefits from participation. Learners become reflective practitioners. Teachers become eager learners. Relationships are nurtured through expansive, all-party involvement as each becomes an equal yet unique participant in the process. Relationship building and the process of shared learning are major elements in the program's content; thus, outcomes extend beyond program-specific knowledge and skills to distinctive person-centered life skills and behaviors.

This theme has major implications for evaluators who find themselves in the middle of nonformal education. When an individual enters the non-formal education experience, that person becomes part of that experience and, regardless of the role he or she had on entering, becomes an equal partner in teaching and learning. This is true for evaluators working in nonformal education who, on entry, may quickly lose their particular identities and related responsibilities. This may sound like a deficit situation, but more often the evaluator gains new, multiple identities, and the associated responsibilities tend to be infinitely greater in number and complexity than originally anticipated.

In fact, in nonformal education program evaluation, the evaluator's role almost always expands to include tasks and responsibilities well beyond traditional boundaries. It is not unusual for most evaluators to facilitate program theory discussions and even to help program staff articulate and record their program's theory. But for evaluators working with nonformal education programs, it is not unusual to help the program staff conceptualize their program as a program, help them identify what elements might appear to be part of any nonformal education program's theory, and then assist with the formulation of their own program's theory.

*Collaborative Adventure.* Nonformal education programs are developed and offered by organizations other than traditional education institutions. Many times, this organization is a newly created collaboration of multiple organizations from the public, nonprofit, or private sectors. Even when a school district or other formal education provider is one of the partners, representatives from the other organizations may be influencing decisions about the program.

The fact that the formal education organization may have little to no influence on program planning, resources, staffing, and evaluation raises some issues. Because the formal education provider has only a limited presence, his or her knowledge of educational principles and practices may well get left in the dust. Instead, the program decision makers are often members of advisory boards and boards of directors who typically have backgrounds related to finance, staffing, program efficiency, and marketing. Because they are far from the education program's front line, not only physically but philosophically, they may be less prepared to make educationally sound decisions regarding programming, focusing more on the bottom line than the front line.

Many organizations that join in partnership to implement nonformal educational programs find themselves there because of an internal or external mandate to broaden their mission to include education or to diversify their services by "doing education." Public agencies are particularly vulnerable to this type of mission creep, and by adding "education" to their services or partnering with others to do so, they believe they are better able to be seen as relevant to clients and funders. Problems arise, though, when these new education services are added but resources are not. Resources used for education are typically redirected away from the major mission areas of the organization, producing perceptions that "education is hijacking 'our' people, budget, and facilities."

## Images for Nonformal Education

Images paint pictures of well-known ideas, which can clarify the unfamiliar. Two images come to mind that relate to evaluating programs in nonformal education settings: the authors' retreat held to create this volume and the series of undeniably ridiculous events that occurred after the retreat, hindering the progress of the volume.

> The Authors' Retreat: Three days in June in the Great Smoky Mountains: Tom, Martha, Julia, David, Nina, Lyn, Cindy, Kate W., Kate C., Nora, Elizabeth, Emma, and John. John was the facilitator. Day One: Hot tub swirling all alone, the fire crackling and spitting, across the valley a lone hawk drifts in the hazy sunlight, Appalachian rockers squeak as quiet conversation competes with the lightly swishing of the leaves overhead. Day Two: Voices raised, brains hurting, darn bees trying for my lemonade, way too many flip chart lists, pretty hot for June—whew, a chorus of pop-tops, hot tub straining with bodies and working overtime, air-hockey anyone? Day Three: Revise the plan and stretch the time line, what's with a guitar player in the dining hall—I'm just looking for coffee, the ticking of the clock overwhelms . . . wish we had more time, cups of coffee outnumber the authors—I hate powdered creamer, is *someone* taking notes? Hugging, waving good-bye, we all promise to stick to deadlines—this volume will be in draft by December 2004.

> After the Retreat: Three authors move—two move across the country; one moves twice; two weather the Florida hurricanes; the lucky ones take vacations; some have family births; some have family deaths; one has her home broken into; children get sick; friends have illnesses; friends pass away; some change jobs; two disappear; one reappears; the other one reappears; they all miss deadlines; editors gently prod again, and again, and again and offer incredible assistance and support. This volume is finished in September 2005.

As life events have recently reminded many of us, our best-laid plans sometimes become unrealistic or impossible to complete, a fate shared by many nonformal education programs. Certainly one small, edited volume cannot answer all the questions related to the evaluation issues of this giant group of stakeholders, constituents, organizational types, programs, and evaluators. But it is a start.

## References

Chenery, L., and Hammerman, W. "Current Practices in the Evaluation of Resident Outdoor Education Programs: Report of a National Survey." *Journal of Environmental Education*, 1984–1985, *16*(2), 35–42.
Childress, R. "Evaluation Strategies and Methodologies Utilized in Public School Environmental Education Programs and Projects—A Report of a National Survey." In

R. Marlett (ed.), *Current Issues in Environmental Education—II: Selected Papers from the Fifth Annual Conference of the National Association for Environmental Education.* Columbus, Ohio: ERIC/SMEAC, 1976.

Civitarese, S., Legg, M., and Zuefle, D. "More Thoughts on the Differences Between Environmental Interpretation and Environmental Education." *Connections, the Environmental Education Section of the National Association for Interpretation,* 1998, 2(1), 3–5.

Coombs, P. H., and Ahmed, M. *Attacking Rural Poverty: How Non-Formal Education Can Help.* Baltimore, Md.: Johns Hopkins University Press, 1974.

Coombs, P. H., Prosser, C., and Ahmed, M. *New Paths to Learning for Rural Children and Youth.* New York: International Council for Educational Development, 1973.

Corporation for Public Broadcasting. *Enhancing Education: A Producer's Guide.* "What Is Educational Outreach?" Available at http://enhancinged.wgbh.org/started/what/index.html. 2002.

Disinger, J. "Environmental Education in the K-12 Schools: A National Survey." In A. Sacks and others (eds.), *Current Issues VII: The Yearbook of Environmental Education and Environmental Studies.* Columbus, Ohio: ERIC/SMEAC, 1981.

Etling, A. "Leadership for Non-formal Education." *Journal of International Agricultural and Extension Education,* 1994, 1(1), 16–24.

Etling, A. *A Toolkit for Volunteer Leaders.* Lincoln, Neb.: UNL Cooperative Extension, 4-H Youth Development, 2003.

Fordham, P. E. "Informal, Non-Formal and Formal Education Programs." In YMCA George Williams College, *ICE301 Lifelong Learning Unit 2.* London: YMCA George Williams College, 1993.

Ham, S. *Environmental Interpretation: A Practical Guide for People with Big Ideas and Small Budgets.* Golden, Colo.: North American Press, 1992.

Kahn, J. *Design of a Workshop to Train P.S.U. Faculty as International Consultants in Youth Development.* University Park: Department of Agriculture and Extension Education, Pennsylvania State University, 1989.

Knapp, D. "Environmental Education and Interpretation for the 21st Century." *Connections, the Environmental Education Section of the National Association for Interpretation,* 1997, 1(2), 3–6.

Marcinkowski, T. "Environmental Education and Interpretation: A Synthesis." *Connections, the Environmental Education Section of the National Association for Interpretation,* 1999, 2(2), 3–6.

Meredith, J. E., Fortner, R. W., and Mullins, G. W. "Model of Affective Learning for Non-Formal Science Education Facilities." *Journal of Research in Science Teaching,* 1997, 34(8), 805–818.

Rogers, A. "Looking Again at Non-Formal and Informal Education—Towards a New Paradigm." In *The Encyclopedia of Informal Education,* 2004. www.infed.org/biblio/non_formal_paradigm.htm. Last updated January 2005.

Sharpe, G. *Interpreting the Environment.* Hoboken, N.J.: Wiley, 1976.

Smith, M. K. (ed.). *The Encyclopedia of Informal Education,* 2005. www.infed.org.

Tilden, F. *Interpreting Our Heritage.* Chapel Hill, N.C.: University of North Carolina Press, 1957.

EMMA NORLAND *is consulting social scientist for the Office of Research and Development at the U.S. Environmental Protection Agency and adjunct professor at the American University School of Public Affairs in the Department of Public Administration.*

2

*This chapter details the wide variety of roles that an evaluator may need to play when evaluating nonformal education programs.*

# I Need a Bigger Suitcase: The Evaluator Role in Nonformal Education

*L. Kate Wiltz*

As the field of program evaluation has evolved, there has been a proliferation of approaches to the craft, each with a different conceptualization of the role the evaluator plays in relation to the program, organization, and practitioners with whom he or she works. Historically, evaluation was characterized as the imposition of a detached set of methods for scrutinizing, and often judging, performance. The mysterious evaluator arrived on site with an academic air of omniscience and wielding the sword of truth. In some cases, this image is still the impression many program practitioners have of evaluators.

Evaluation can be, and sometimes is, effectively restricted to the determination of quality within a program (Scriven, 1991; Stufflebeam, 1994). Here the evaluator role is one of technical specialist or judge. However, the evaluation field is replete with kinder, gentler, and broader options for program evaluation and the related services of program development, training, and improvement. Participatory, empowerment, democratic, utilization-focused, and other stakeholder-based approaches offer alternative roles for an evaluator working with program teams for a variety of purposes related to improving or assessing programs.

A few recent conceptualizations of evaluator role include that of a "critical friend" (Rallis and Rossman, 2000), an educator who fosters dialogue, reflection, and inquiry (Morabito, 2002), a member of the program team providing an evaluation perspective (Patton, 1997), and an advocate for social change (Morabito, 2002; Patton, 1997). In nonformal education, with

NEW DIRECTIONS FOR EVALUATION, no. 108, Winter 2005   © Wiley Periodicals, Inc.
Published online in Wiley InterScience (www.interscience.wiley.com) • DOI: 10.1002/ev.168

its highly variable program contexts and nontraditional approaches to teaching and learning, some of these alternative evaluator roles are well suited to programs embarking on formal evaluation projects.

With so many potential roles to play in an evaluation project, both evaluators and program practitioners must carefully reflect on their values and the needs of their program when considering formalized evaluation. Program teams embarking on evaluation often cite objectivity and credibility as the primary qualities they are seeking from an evaluator. These qualities are fundamental expectations of any evaluation (although their contextual meanings should be explored for any given program). Much more variable and important to the success of the evaluation is the role that program teams would like the evaluator to play in the ensuing evaluation relationship. Do they expect a partner or collaborator? A technical specialist? A facilitator or guide for exploring the nature and meaning of their work? Of course, the evaluator is not a blank slate whose role is defined exclusively by clients. Factors affecting the evaluator role are a complicated mix of program, people, setting, and culture.

The role of the evaluator has been characterized as both "stance" and "strategy" (Schwandt, 2001). That is, the evaluator's role can be thought of as an interplay of personal identity and interpersonal relationships, as well as the function or the set of behaviors this person employs in providing a service. These relationships and actions are contextual. While some of the variables that shape the role of the evaluator in any given project are personal, such as the values, ethics, skills, and talents of the evaluator and clients, other variables are situationally defined and emerge from the structure and function of the organization within which the program is housed and the history and politics of the program (Patton, 1997).

This chapter highlights and explores two common and important characteristics of evaluation that shape the relationships and contexts—and the key roles evaluators play—in the field of nonformal environmental education. First, for a variety of reasons emerging from the history of nonformal education and the backgrounds of those working in environmental education, evaluations in this setting tend to require preevaluation activities. These activities are necessary to prepare the program, the practitioners, and the organization for an evaluation and the subsequent application of its findings.

Second, the relationships among evaluators and program practitioners and stakeholders in the nonformal environmental education setting tend to be more personal than traditional evaluator-client relationships. These two aspects of nonformal environmental education evaluation—more intensive developmental activities and closer relationships with program practitioners—present a number of opportunities as well as potential pitfalls for the evaluator in navigating the evaluation relationships and activities in context. The thoughtful evaluator must be attentive to the management of role boundaries throughout each evaluation project.

New Directions for Evaluation • DOI 10.1002/ev

While my own experiences and the examples I use here are drawn from the nonformal fields of environmental and agricultural education as well as natural resources interpretation, I hope that the illustrations and points apply to those working across the many nonformal education disciplines. Therefore, I use the term *nonformal education* inclusively throughout the chapter.

## Being Up-Front About Evaluation

As nonformal organizations and programs embark on evaluation, the process is consistently and necessarily front-loaded with preevaluation activities. Regardless of the apparent maturity of the program, the evaluator is repeatedly compelled to postpone evaluation in the strictest sense, instead responding to the need for more up-front activities to prepare the program team (and the evaluator) for the evaluation and subsequent use of its results. A number of factors that set nonformal education apart from formal education call for investment on the part of both the evaluator and the program practitioners. These activities shape the course of the evaluation relationship and call for flexibility in the roles of the evaluator.

In a recent cluster evaluation of a multisite park-based education program, it was discovered in the initial stages of the project that several sites had virtually no program. They lacked the resources, knowledge, and skills required to get their program up and running. (At one site, the park educator position was unfilled, and the secretary was leading the program.) Prior to beginning work on the evaluation itself, the evaluation team recommended that these sites receive some program development assistance. The client requested that the evaluation team coordinate a series of program development site visits. The evaluators used their expertise in program development to work with the local teams to (re)design and implement their programs. Extra time was taken at this early point in the evaluation relationship to educate and assist disadvantaged program sites. The result for the park system was more effective programming. The result for the evaluation was a richer base from which to draw data for understanding the conditions that favored program success.

Unlike formal education, most nonformal programs lack a connection to the world of evaluation thinking and methods. Formal education and evaluation have a long-standing relationship. Formal education training programs often include courses in evaluation, program development, and research methodology. Nonformal education has not shared this history. Its practitioners are not typically trained in education. Their work outside the scrutinizing eye of public oversight (with a few recent exceptions falling under the 1993 Government Performance and Results Act) has resulted in its practitioners' unfamiliarity with and even fear of evaluation.

Evaluators of nonformal programs therefore must make a concerted effort to win over their clients, who have frequently had little exposure to

New Directions for Evaluation • DOI 10.1002/ev

formalized evaluation. Time spent in building mutual trust and respect for the evaluator's expertise and its benefits to programming is essential to maximizing use of subsequent evaluation activities. Evaluators in these settings often find themselves assuming roles such as facilitator, educator, and adviser at this preevaluation stage.

**Facilitator.** Nonformal education practitioners frequently are not educators by formal training. In fact, arriving at a program team meeting, the evaluator is likely to find representation from such disparate fields as ecology, art, history, chemistry, communications, business administration, natural history, and social services. These diverse stakeholders (and these are just the program staff) are often enthusiastic and united by their common dedication to a particular place or issue, but they frequently have different understandings of their program and its purpose or goals, not to mention evaluation. Before an evaluation can begin to look at program function or outcomes, the terms need to be explored and defined within the core program team. These activities require the evaluator to take on a facilitator role in which he or she poses questions, guides discussion, and enables the program team to come to a common understanding of their program, often reshaping their expectations about their program and evaluation. "This role requires that the evaluator immerse herself/himself into the deliberations concerning the program while avoiding input that would shift the ownership for the program away from clients" (Shula, 2001, p. 112).

**Content Expert and Educator.** Many nonformal education programs are working toward goals that present difficulties when translating them into measurable outcomes for evaluation. Sometimes the goals are not well developed; sometimes they are entirely affective in nature; frequently they are broad, long-term goals that could take years to achieve. Employing evaluability assessment, explicating program theory, and applying logic modeling can assist program teams in clarifying their purpose and stating their specific program goals. Each of these techniques draws from research to support program methods and link goals, outcomes, and impact.

This body of research is typically rooted in the program's content discipline. For example, a residential outdoor education program's logic model could cite the research on residential learning and outdoor education to support its chosen program activities and anticipated outcomes. However, practitioners are often unfamiliar with the applicable literature to support their program goals and methods. In addition, the research base for environmental education in nonformal settings is relatively undeveloped, and work in the field relies largely on other disciplines.

While the evaluability assessment process can be informed by empirical data from the implementation stages of the program (Shula, 2001) and other similar programs, the variability across program sites, audiences, and content makes this project cross-pollination difficult. Therefore, nonformal education evaluators are often looked to as resources on the applicable literature. More than once an evaluator has arrived on the scene to be met with the complaint by a nonformal educator that her exhaustive search for an instrument to measure program outcomes has failed: "Nobody has ever done a geology program with a day-long introductory lecture, four half-day field visits, two overnight trips, journaling and therapeutic rock polishing with disadvantaged youth from rural Appalachia!" In this context, the evaluator may assume a teaching stance with respect to his clients.

The variability across nonformal education programs has also made the creation of standards of practice, and therefore measurement criteria, more complicated. In nonformal education programs, there is often a strong conviction among practitioners about the right way to implement programming, but it is accompanied by a sense that their "unique constellation of conditions" (Patton, 1998, p. 160) overwhelms most generalizations that can be made about practice in the field.

For example, the program director of an urban after-school day camp can have a hard time seeing similarities between his program and that of a remote park-based residential learning center, even if their programs have similar activities and desired outcomes for students. In fact, there are standards of practice in many nonformal education fields, including environmental education, and they are variously well developed and employed across their respective fields. Recently published guidelines for nonformal environmental education (North American Association for Environmental Education, 2004) provide a valuable tool for the evaluator. In this setting, it is often the evaluator who is familiarizing the practitioners with the emerging literature on better practices in their field. The evaluator as educator is not a new role (see Cronbach and others, 1980), but this expanded instructional role requires that in addition to evaluation and program development, the evaluator be more intimately familiar with the literature of the discipline, such as that of alternative and environmental education.

**Internal Adviser.** Another aspect of nonformal education programs that presents an opportunity for up-front evaluation services is the interconnectedness of the programs within and across organizations. Scarce resources and mutual goals have fostered a proliferation of partnerships in nonformal education in which programs are bundled with others from partnering agencies to work in concert toward long-term outcomes. Often a program is part of a suite of activities conducted across an organization to achieve mission-stated goals. Programs are more fully understood in their organizational context, and individual program evaluations mandated by a funder often lack the resources to address system issues that affect program performance. In this setting, explication of the relationships among programs and organizations is critical to an effective evaluation. When possible, a successful evaluation relationship is that of a long-term partnership between the evaluator and organization (Mathison, 1994) with a focus on organizational learning. The evaluator in these settings crosses boundaries, acting often like an internal evaluator who advises program administrators and highlights organizational issues affecting program delivery.

**The Sum of the Parts.** In addition to some of the functional uniqueness of nonformal education, there are cultural differences that require attention from and shape interactions with the program evaluator. Nonformal environmental education programs often take place in a leisure setting. Their participants are noncaptive learners, directing their own course of study and often viewing their participation in terms of recreation as opposed to education (Knudson, Cable, and Beck, 1999). The nonformal education program in this way is supplemental education, not compulsory. Learners come to the program with a variety of personal goals surrounding their experience (for example, having fun, learning the names of birds, relaxation, and exercise, among many others) and, in many cases, an immense diversity of backgrounds and life experiences.

Nonformal education staff add to these learner-directed goals other desired outcomes for the participants, including stewardship of natural and cultural resources, a sense of place, understanding of and appreciation of biodiversity, and responsible environmental behavior, to name a few. It is not unheard of, for instance, for a program such as a family creek hike to have among its goals the lofty aim of affecting the participants' future choices at the polling booth.

In part because participants can go elsewhere at any time, nonformal education has become creative in its approach to programming in an effort to engage participants and incorporate learner-centered goals into the programs. The result is a sort of program gestalt in which program variables such as setting, presentation of content, articulation of unifying themes, and coordination of activities are expected to have a synergistic effect. While nonformal education programs incorporate strategies from traditional pedagogy as well as experiential and transformative learning, there is an expectation that participants will achieve some benefits from the program process itself. That is, the program is intended to have impact derived from the participant experience beyond that of the content and activities.

Frequently a hike in the woods with specific learning objectives (affective and cognitive) relies on the participants' making connections with the content in some unique, affective ways. Participants expressing a sense of place or feelings of stewardship after the program may have widely varying (but inextricably related) intermediate feelings such as patriotism, peacefulness, affinity to the earth or one's heritage, deep admiration, or awe. In evaluation terms, these types of outcomes are often labeled "unanticipated," for they are not always articulated in the formal program strategy. Nevertheless, they are a foundational element of the program's process. The alternative approaches and settings of nonformal education are intended to foster often very personal outcomes in each of the participants (see Tilden, 1977).

Tilden, in his instrumental work on the field of interpretation, instructs that the educator at times does best not to speak at all when presenting particularly meaningful sites or artifacts. This kind of education "aims not to *do something* to the listener, but *to provoke the listener to do something to himself*" (Tilden, 1977, p. 111). The nonformal educator can and should pause to allow the learners to connect with the resource (language such as this is the basis of many park-based programs). At the foot of El Capitan, in the middle of a battlefield cemetery, at the site where humans first took flight, or in view of a canyon carved by an ancient river, information is essential to the educational program. Ultimately, though, it is the program participants' relationship with the setting that infuses the information with meaning. It is this meaning around which many nonformal education programs build their objectives. Program participants could learn about watersheds anywhere, but the same information conveyed as they traverse a creek from its headwaters to mouth imbues the program with innumerable affective outcomes that are inherent to the nonformal experience.

For the evaluator, the relevance of this culture of program gestalt is its inherent compatibility with evaluation process use and influence as described by Patton (1997), Morobito (2002), and others. Nonformal education program teams frequently expect, and require from their evaluators, more than summative judgments or formative findings. The evaluator in these settings is compelled to employ participatory approaches that facilitate learning among stakeholders and can be remarkably similar to the experiential approaches employed by the practitioners in their programming. Fostering dialogue, reflection, and inquiry in an effort to allow stakeholders to identify and clarify beliefs and assumptions about their program is key to process influence in evaluation and enhances evaluation use and organizational learning (Morobito, 2002).

Process use emerges from the evaluator's calling to prioritize the use of evaluation and a belief in the benefits of evaluative thinking for program and organizational development. It is the value-added in evaluation practice and is critical in fields like nonformal education in which scarce resources and a newness to evaluation have restricted opportunities for this type of formalized reflective practice. The imperative is for these nonformal education teams to come away with more than an evaluation of their program and to have been changed in a way that will have an impact on the ways in which they do their jobs in the future.

**The Context for Evaluation.** The previous section described attributes of nonformal education that create a context conducive to up-front evaluation or program development activities. These attributes act on the aspect of evaluator role that is his "actions in context" or his "strategy"—the things he chooses to do or the approaches he takes in his practice of evaluation. The attention to participatory approaches and clarifying program teams' understandings of the program's theory require the evaluator to take an expansive view of this craft. The evaluator roles alluded to here are those of educator, facilitator, content expert, or even organizational consultant, internal evaluator, or program advocate, all with an emphasis on program or organizational improvement. These roles, and the participatory and stakeholder-based processes they incorporate, often call for a number of activities that are not explored in the original evaluation contract. As program and team needs emerge and are attended to spontaneously, problems can arise for the evaluator who is attempting to maintain an appropriate level of immersion in the activities of the program team (Stake, 2004).

## Getting (Too?) Close

A second characteristic of nonformal education program evaluation is that the relationships tend to be closer than the usual professional interactions. Evaluator and program team are often drawn into relationships characterized by such terms as *friend, partner,* and *collaborator.* These roles emerge in part from the extra time spent with program practitioners in the pre-evaluation phases of the relationship, but also from the conditions of the nonformal setting that often send the evaluator on a journey, literally, as he or she is coming to understand the program.

> Having spent the day in the field, with only the branches of the tall trees protecting them from the pouring rain, the last of the woodland owners pulled away from the tree farm hanging his drenched arm out the car window in a parting wave. The evaluator stood with the program staff next to the woods, holding his soggy notebook and a stack of completed participant feedback forms. As they hopped into the two cars that had caravanned to the remote site, the subject of grabbing dinner before the two-hour drive back to the university was raised. All were in favor, and the search was on for any restaurant that did not also sell gasoline. The evaluator looked forlornly at his boots and mused aloud about the small pleasures of dry socks. Quickly the driver of the car reached into the glove box and presented him with a fresh pair. "Never leave home without them!"

The relationships the evaluator creates with program practitioners and other stakeholders frame his activities and in many ways have an impact on evaluation use more than the activities themselves. There are several factors operating in nonformal education programs that promote closer-than-average relationships among the evaluation participants. These include the nonformal education roots of many evaluators practicing in the field today, a culture of role fluidity among nonformal education practitioners, and the alternative settings and methodologies of nonformal education.

**Entangled Roots.** A few generalizations can be made about nonformal education program evaluators. Most have strong ties to their contextual field of interest. In fact, many came to evaluation by way of nonformal education, having recognized a need in the field for evaluation. They were first nonformal educators, then evaluators. As such they share many of the values surrounding education and, in the case of environmental education, values pertaining to natural and cultural resources with program practitioners. These nonformal evaluators believe in the programs—the foundational theories, approaches, and messages—with which they work. They also tend to limit their evaluation practice to the nonformal education field.

This close relationship with program content can inform evaluators who take on a consultative or remediation role in evaluations, and certainly the cultural and language factors that can be difficult for evaluators to navigate pose less of a barrier for these evaluators. However, Mathison (1991) warns that role definition can be complicated by an evaluator's association with his "contextual discipline of practice" and points to specific concerns about appropriate methodologies and which guidelines to consult for continuing education and standards of practice for the evaluator.

If not attended to overtly, the shared values among program evaluators and practitioners in these settings could present a barrier to the critical stance inherent in evaluation. However, it is also likely that a strong background in the research and practice that supports nonformal education imbues the evaluator with a keen eye for both the negative and positive—for seeing what is working and what is not in a given context. It is incumbent upon the evaluator to take into consideration Stake's admonishment that "a contract to discern quality is *not* a license to fix things" (2004, p. 105). When an evaluator has direct experience in nonformal education programming, this line between evaluation and remediation can be particularly difficult to navigate. Some contexts, such as when the evaluator's experience provides programming insight that is not contained among the members of the program team itself, call for the evaluator to act in a consultant role, at times interpreting findings into options for future program strategy in order to facilitate use of the results. However, these circumstances require the evaluator to present options and educate stakeholders, as opposed to directing and prescribing application of the findings.

Regardless of the evaluator's connection to nonformal education, evaluation's recent attention to social betterment (King and Stevahn, 2002) makes it likely that the evaluator will share a commitment to the ideals of the organizations and programs with which she works. Caring about the program, or what Stake (2004) calls a "confluence of interest," does not necessarily constitute bias (Scriven, 1993), and in fact it has been characterized as a necessary component of a successful evaluator-client relationship (Mathison, 1994). These shared values can foster mutual respect and trust between an evaluator and other stakeholders, enabling higher levels of learning (Rallis and Rossman, 2000) and use (Patton, 1997). However, confluence of interest may not be fully descriptive of the type of relationship that nonformal evaluators have with their programs. At times, it is more aptly a confluence of spirit. As evaluators who want their work to "contribute to the making of a better world" (Stake, 2004, p. 103), those working in nonformal education often see their role in terms of supporting a set of ideals. When faced with a successful program that is doing good work, the temptation for the evaluator to move into the role of cheerleader or public relations consultant can be great.

> As I listened, I couldn't believe the fantastic things I kept hearing about this new program. They seemed to be doing all the right things, and I was thrilled with the opportunity to work with a partnership involving a major metropolitan museum, three school districts, and eight state and local agencies. As we discussed the specifics of the program team's needs regarding the evaluation, my heart began to grow wary. The museum administrators were clear about their motivations for the evaluation: while they wanted data for program improvement, the primary product had to be a public relations piece to use in advertising the program's success to potential funders. The evaluator needed to present the data in a glossy full-color format "highlighting our success with the schools." Were the evaluation and I going to be a pawn in a political grab for money? How could I fairly gather and present data for program improvement, given their desired format for the final report? But as they came to understand my conflict and I became familiar with their formative needs, we were able to draw up a two-part contract in which the data were first shared and interpreted with the program team and subsequently pulled into a marketing publication (not an evaluation report) highlighting program successes.

In situations such as this one when program teams are looking for a public relations product from their evaluation, the evaluator must be careful to delineate the boundaries between reporting evaluation information and creating marketing materials based on evaluation findings.

**"Role-ing" with It.** Another factor in the nonformal evaluator-client relationship is the relative fluidity of roles that is commonly accepted in the nonformal education culture. Roles in formal education are usually clearly defined and well delineated; although administrators typically have teaching experience, an elementary teacher does not teach the occasional tenth-grade algebra class, and the school psychologist does not write science curriculum. In nonformal education, roles are more tenuous and are often defined by an individual's skills as they become apparent or are based on the needs of the project at hand as opposed to one's job title. There is a conscious spirit of the collective effort to accomplish a mission.

Perhaps driven by the lean budgets and unusual circumstances of nonformal education programming, it is in this setting that one repeatedly will find the proverbial "all hands pitching in" to get something done. The nonformal education evaluator, particularly one with experience in the field, inevitably will be asked to perform nonevaluative activities. These may range from the more benign appeal for advice in an administrator's question, "What would you do here?" to a spontaneous request to assist in program delivery.

> I arrived, pen and data collection sheet in hand, ready to observe the 4H'ers in their stream ecology field experience. As the kids accumulated on the stream bank, I became acutely aware of an imbalance. The adults were not outnumbered in the usual ratios; there was a definite lack of educators in this mix. Before I knew what was happening, I was handed a kit and pointed to a spot downstream. "Here. You know macroinvertebrates. Take this group and run through the IBI [biotic index] worksheet with them."

While this example may seem extreme, to a program practitioner whose main concern is delivering the best learning experience possible on a given day, asking the evaluator to contribute directly to the program does not seem like an infringement on role identity. Situations often arise within a project that call on evaluators to spontaneously reexamine and renegotiate their role with certain ethical implications (Schwandt, 2001; Newman and Brown, 1996; Kirkhart and others, 1979). In nonformal education, such requests are part of making programming work.

**Bonding Experiences.** Just as immersion in sublime environs or challenge-based activities leads to a program gestalt for participants, a sense of shared adventure often enriches the evaluator-practitioner relationship. The nonformal setting blurs the professional and informal. It is hard to maintain any degree of separation from a program during which you ford creeks, climb mountains, and fell trees—and that was just to get to the program site. By the time the evaluator gets to the program, a sense of camaraderie has developed with the program staff that is difficult to ignore. That bonding is often the goal of a program. The practitioners and evaluator have fallen prey to the program's "intended unintentional" benefits.

> My partner and I climbed into the small SUV driven by the park's director of education and accompanied by one of the rangers. We set out to tour the site and get a feel for the meanings and messages of the park's resources. As we buckled up, our guide said cheerfully, "Don't worry about the quicksand—there have already been a couple of folks in the canyon this spring, so we shouldn't hit any surprises." What? We looked across the back seat at each other with a combination of bewilderment and panic in our eyes. "Yeah," he continued, "the pockets of quicksand have swallowed entire vehicles. They move each year as the rains flood the canyon floor, so we're careful to follow the tracks of the private tour guides that start early in the spring. Just don't want to be driving around at night where we might stray off the path." The threat of succumbing to quicksand added an adventuresome flair to our afternoon exploration to be

sure. Later, having basked in the beauty and wonder of the petroglyph-covered rock walls and listened to stories of ancient and modern canyon inhabitants, we returned to our car from a brief stop to discover one completely flat tire and a somewhat distraught ranger: "Ladies, I'm afraid we don't have a spare." Although the hour was not late, I glanced up as the sun was disappearing behind the steep canyon walls. Thank goodness for dispatch radios!

**Oh, and One More Thing.** The close relationships that emerge from shared experiences in alternative venues can enhance many of the evaluation-related activities that depend on trust and respect for maximized benefit. It can be challenging, and sometimes threatening, for practitioners to allow evaluators into their program decision-making process, and mutual trust and respect create a more collegial atmosphere in which honest reflection on program purpose and outcomes is possible. These same relationships can result in difficult decisions surrounding questions of limits to professional commitment. Particularly with an evaluation in which the process and findings have more impact than anticipated, the evaluator can find herself faced with the "just one more thing" syndrome. Excited about the application of the evaluation activities, there arises a temptation (sometimes a direct request) to add on to the end of a project, working beyond the contractual agreement. Often program teams that have seen the benefits of empirically based decision making are enthusiastic about putting more measures in place in their new evaluation system or tailoring the summary report for yet another audience. When the financial support has run out for the evaluation activities, as it usually does in the nonformal world of one-time and patchwork funding, it can be difficult for the committed and involved evaluator to disregard requests such as these, particularly when they come from friends.

A number of strategies can assist evaluators in supporting the programs they evaluate beyond the evaluation contract, while preserving their professional (and financial) independence. Practicing an adaptive and reactive approach to evaluation (Patton, 1997) and responsively addressing the emerging needs of the stakeholders as new uses become apparent can head off the "one more thing" syndrome before it arises. This approach allows evaluators to renegotiate the processes and products as the program team learns more about their program and their evaluation needs and wants. In addition, formalizing a longer-term partnership with the client organization may be possible and certainly beneficial to programs housed in larger establishments (Mathison, 1994).

## Managing Boundaries

The ways in which nonformal education programs elicit relatively close relationships among their evaluation participants and the programs' needs for a variety of evaluation and consultation services raise questions about the propriety and management of the roles an evaluator plays in these settings. Scriven (1997) has warned against the ethical dangers of close relationships in evaluation, indicating the potential for these relationships to cloud the evaluator's ability to identify and interpret negative findings.

The up-front evaluation activities frequently called for in nonformal program settings benefit from and foster close relationships. However, they can present a conflict of interest for the evaluator who presumes to evaluate those same programs—"not a financial or personal conflict of interest, but a conflict between the close involvement required of an evaluation consultant and what Scriven calls 'the distanced ideal' required of an evaluator" (Hendricks, 2001, p. 109). In addition, the evaluator holds a lot of power to shape the program of interest and must be careful not to abuse that power. Some believe that providing developmental services to program teams is in itself an abuse; several evaluators have admonished those who mix evaluation consultation roles with performing evaluations of the same program (Scriven, 1991; Stufflebeam, 1994; Stake, 2004).

So what is the evaluation team to do? Key to operating ethically in nonformal education evaluation is understanding and matching the clients' expectations and needs with the evaluator's ability and willingness to meet them. Subsequently the evaluator and program practitioners must maximize the opportunities for up-front services and closer relationships while respecting the roles that have been defined for each other. This requires effort on the part of both the evaluator and practitioner to refrain from role slippage (Mark, 2002) when it is not the intent of both parties for a new role to emerge. As Hendricks warned from the evaluator perspective, "There's something about human nature that makes it hard to avoid helping good people when you're all together in the same room" (2001, p. 109).

Role negotiation must be explicit and ongoing, with opportunities for adjustment when necessary. Patton (1997, 1998) has advocated situational evaluation, with its requisite attention to the specific conditions of each new program that can have an impact on use of the evaluation. As an evaluator steps into a particular nonformal program environment, the process of becoming familiar with the program, its players, and its culture begins. Concurrently, the program team is embarking on a similar learning experience.

As evaluators, we owe it to our clients to clarify our stance and strategy in our work, present alternatives where we see them, and educate where necessary to enable clientele to make choices about their program. It is during this time that ideas are often challenged about how a program is working and how evaluation can inform the program and organization. This period of introduction and exploration is followed by "The Talk," that is, getting to know each other is not enough. The evaluator must be willing to educate clients about the options for evaluation services and his willingness and ability to provide those services (Patton, 1997). Subsequently the duties, expectations, and responsibilities—the functional aspect of the role concept—should be explicitly negotiated and renegotiated when necessary as the project evolves (Morobito, 2002; Patton, 1997; Newman and Brown, 1996; Korr, 1982).

A word of caution is necessary, though, for when the evaluator presents a suite of options to the program team as Patton (1997) describes, there is a risk of the client's acquiescing to the evaluator's advice, no matter how unbiased a presentation is made: the "what would you do?" scenario. Using Patton's menu of evaluation services metaphor, how many of us have ever asked the seemingly competent waiter to recommend something from the menu?

It takes skill to offer the appropriate guidance and foster the clients' decision making at these early stages. For instance, there are clearly times when the evaluator will come up with options for a team that he or she is not able or willing to perform. Perhaps to maintain objectivity in a summative situation, he wants to opt out of developmental activities in the near term; perhaps the client is leaning toward methodologies or approaches that are not comfortable for the evaluator. The evaluator could be heard saying, "Here are some of the best options for your program [situation]. I can do x, y, or z with you, but a or b would probably require you to hire a different evaluator." A not unimaginable response would be, "But we finally found an evaluator who understands us! We want you to do it! We'll do it your way." More important than the nature of the roles and services is the clear understanding of the advantages and disadvantages of choices made in crafting the evaluation relationship. This type of reflective practice must be infused into any role played by either the evaluator or program practitioners.

Nonformal education program evaluators will find themselves putting on many hats and redefining themselves as they work in the variety of nonformal program contexts. These evaluators must consider the implications of the relationships they develop and activities they pursue with their program teams if they are to provide ethical and appropriate evaluation services to their clients. As both nonformal educators and evaluators clarify their stance and strategy, they are guided by a reflective practice in which the evaluator embraces what is perhaps an overarching role: that of nonformal educator.

The evaluator as nonformal educator provides clients with opportunities for learning suited to their interests and preferences and then guides them as they are introduced to new information and points of decision. This evaluator allows the "learners" to direct their learning and own both the process and product of evaluation. This evaluator sees connections among evaluation participants and program components and facilitates understanding. This evaluator sits at the table providing an evaluation perspective to programming when necessary, offers recommendations as a critical friend, or embarks on the evaluation journey as a partner. In evaluating nonformal education, the roles will emerge and evolve whether we want them to or not, so one final word of advice: remember to bring an extra suitcase for all the hats.

## References

Cronbach, C. J., and others. *Toward Reform of Program Evaluation.* San Francisco: Jossey-Bass, 1980.

Hendricks, M. "Commentary: Dear Eva." *American Journal of Evaluation,* 2001, 22(1), 108–110.

King, J. A., and Stevahn, L. "Three Frameworks for Considering Evaluator Role." In K. E. Ryan and T. A. Schwandt (eds.), *Exploring Evaluator Role and Identity: A Volume in Evaluation and Society.* Greenwich, Conn.: Information Age, 2002.

Kirkhart, K. E., and others. *The "By the Way . . . " Phenomenon: Role Redefinition in Program Evaluation,* 1979 (ED201647). http://www.eric.ed.gov/ERICWebPortal/Home. portal?_nfpb=true&ERICExtSearch_SearchValue_0=Kirkhart&ERICExtSearch_Searc hType_0=au&_pageLabel=RecordDetails&objectId=0900000b80114ac8.

Knudson, D. M., Cable, T. T., and Beck, L. *Interpretation of Cultural and Natural Resources.* State College, Pa.: Venture Publishing, 1999.

Korr, W. S. "How Evaluators Can Deal with Role Conflict." *Evaluation and Program Planning: An International Journal,* 1982, 5(1), 53–58.

Mark, M. M. "Toward Better Understanding of Evaluator Roles. In K. E. Ryan and T. A. Schwandt (eds.), *Exploring Evaluator Role and Identity: A Volume in Evaluation and Society.* Greenwich, Conn.: Information Age, 2002.

Mathison, S. "Role Conflicts for Internal Evaluators." *Evaluation and Program Planning,* 1991, 14, 173–179.

Mathison, S. "Rethinking the Evaluator Role: Partnerships Between Organizations and Evaluators." *Evaluation and Program Planning,* 1994, 17(3), 299–304.

Morabito, S. "Evaluator Roles and Strategies for Expanding Evaluation Process Influence." *American Journal of Evaluation,* 2002, 23(3), 321–330.

Newman, D. L., and Brown, R. D. *Applied Ethics for Program Evaluation.* Thousand Oaks, Calif.: Sage, 1996.

North American Association for Environmental Education. *Nonformal Environmental Education Programs: Guidelines for Excellence.* Washington, D.C.: North American Association for Environmental Education, 2004.

Patton, M. Q. *Utilization-Focused Evaluation: A New Century Text.* (3rd ed.) Thousand Oaks, Calif.: Sage, 1997.

Patton, M. Q. "The Challenges of Diversity in Evaluation." *Science Communication,* 1998, 20(1), 148–164.

Rallis, S. F., and Rossman, G. B. "Dialogue for Learning: Evaluator as Critical Friend." In R. K. Hopson (ed.), *How and Why Language Matters in Evaluation.* New Directions for Evaluation, no. 86. San Francisco: Jossey-Bass, 2000.

Schwandt, T. A. "Responsiveness and Everyday Life." In J. C. Greene and T. A. Abma (eds.), *Responsive Evaluation.* New Directions for Evaluation, no. 92. San Francisco: Jossey-Bass, 2001.

Scriven, M. "Beyond Formative and Summative Evaluation." In M. W. McLaughlin and D. C. Phillips (eds.), *Evaluation and Education: At Quarter Century.* Chicago: University of Chicago Press, 1991.

Scriven, M. (ed.). *Hard-Won Lessons in Program Evaluation.* New Directions for Program Evaluation, no. 58. San Francisco: Jossey-Bass, 1993.

Scriven, M. "Truth and Objectivity in Evaluation." In E. Chelimsky and W. R. Shadish (eds.), *Evaluation for the 21st Century: A Handbook.* Thousand Oaks, Calif.: Sage, 1997.

Shula, L. M. "Commentary: 'Tinker, Tailor, Soldier, Sailor': The Evaluator Role in High Stakes Program Design." *American Journal of Evaluation,* 2001, 22(1), 111–115.

Stake, B. "How Far Dare an Evaluator Go Toward Saving the World?" *American Journal of Evaluation,* 2004, 25(1), 103–107.

Stufflebeam, D. "Empowerment Evaluation, Objectivist Evaluation, and Evaluation Standards: Where the Future of Evaluation Should Not Go and Where It Needs to Go." *Evaluation Practice,* 1994, 15(3), 321–338.

Tilden, F. *Interpreting Our Heritage.* (3rd ed.) Chapel Hill: University of North Carolina Press, 1977.

*L. KATE WILTZ currently resides in Somerset, Kentucky, and provides evaluation services to Ohio State University Extension programs in the School of Environment and Natural Resources.*

3

*This chapter reviews the development of an evaluation system by focusing on the varied and intensive roles that stakeholders played throughout the creation of an entire evaluation process.*

# Evaluation of the Wonders in Nature–Wonders in Neighborhoods Conservation Education Program: Stakeholders Gone Wild!

*Cindy Somers*

Over the past twenty years, stakeholder participation in the planning and implementation of natural resource and environmental management plans has become increasingly more common (Selin and Chavez, 1995; Wondolleck and Yaffee, 2000). In conjunction with the increased focus on obtaining wide participation (getting input from as many interested parties as possible), understanding the importance of the ways in which stakeholders can contribute to the management of public resources has grown as well. Over time, opportunities for stakeholder involvement have increased from short-term, fairly detached interactions such as public hearings and comment periods to much longer, more in-depth collaborative undertakings that include a variety of stakeholder groups in all phases of development, implementation, and evaluation of management plans (Blahna and Yonts-Shepard, 1989; Bentrup, 2001).

This trend toward more in-depth, stakeholder-directed involvement in the management of natural resources coincides with a similar development

I acknowledge and thank the members of the evaluation team who made this project the success that it was. The team from the Ohio State University with whom I worked consisted of Emma Norland, School of Educational Policy and Leadership; Joe Heimlich, School of Natural Resources; and Claudia Figueiredo, graduate student in the School of Educational Policy and Leadership. It was truly a team effort.

in the field of environmental education. Evidence of this movement can be found in the guidelines of the North American Association for Environmental Education (1999, 2004) for formal and nonformal environmental education, both of which strongly emphasize the importance of learner-focused and audience-directed educational experiences. These guidelines, along with a variety of other forces, are influencing many environmental education programs to change the way they develop and implement their programs. As a result, program participants and other stakeholders are becoming increasingly involved in determining the objectives, content, and execution of the programs in which they participate.

Unfortunately, this trend in stakeholder involvement has not been as evident in the evaluation of conservation and environmental education programs. As illustrated by recent publications directed at providers of nonformal education in a variety of settings, there is growing awareness of the importance of evaluation (Committee on Audience Research and Evaluation, 1997; Diamond, 1999; Frechtling, 1995, 2002; Thomson and Hoffman, 2004; McCurley and Vineyard, 2003; North American Association for Environmental Education, 2004). Despite this realization, however, there are still few programs that are formally evaluated. Furthermore, as with many other conservation initiatives, the few programs that are evaluated tend to follow a traditional model of distanced evaluation where evaluators have limited contact with stakeholders. In most cases, external evaluators or academic researchers are called in to conduct an evaluation with the goal of fulfilling a grant requirement or to provide evidence of accountability rather than produce data for use in improving the program. As McDuff (2002) points out, "In these evaluations, local stakeholders are involved as data sources through interviews and surveys, for example, but not as data collectors or evaluation designers" (p. 25).

The participatory evaluation approach is more directed to the specific concerns and needs of program stakeholders. Although a wide range of specific techniques, goals, and levels of stakeholder involvement falls under the label "participatory evaluation" (see Whitmore, 1998), one of the key principles underlying the approach is that "the evaluation must involve and be useful to the program's end users" (Burke, 1998, p. 44). There are very few examples in the literature of evaluations of conservation education programs that have used a stakeholder-based, participatory approach. The development and implementation of the Wonders in Nature–Wonders in Neighborhoods (W.I.N.–W.I.N.) evaluation system provides just such an example.

## Background

W.I.N.–W.I.N. has been providing wildlife-related conservation education to schoolchildren throughout the Denver metropolitan area since 1996. Specifically designed for students in early childhood education classes

through fifth grade, W.I.N.–W.I.N. is intended to heighten children's awareness and understanding of the natural world. The program has an interdis-
ciplinary and multifaceted curriculum that aims to "foster an appreciation
of wildlife and their habitats and the conservation of these natural resources
through a variety of wildlife-related learning experiences" (Denver Zoological Foundation, 2000).

At the time of the evaluation, teachers and children from more than
two dozen schools were participating in the program. These schools were
located in ethnically and culturally diverse urban neighborhoods in and
around the city of Denver. To ensure access and affordability, W.I.N.–
W.I.N. paid for all expenses and offered the program at no cost to the
selected schools. In addition, the program provided materials and instruction (when appropriate) in both English and Spanish, and teachers received
training in how to implement the activities and incorporate W.I.N.–W.I.N.
into their class curriculum.

The program consists of five primary components that link together to
provide students with a variety of educational experiences related to nature
and wildlife:

- Four to seven in-class lessons provided by a W.I.N.–W.I.N. instructor
- Sets of pre- and postvisit activities that correlate with each of the in-class
  lessons and are to be taught by the classroom teacher
- One or two field site visits to environmental or wildlife-related locations
  and facilities throughout the Denver metropolitan area and Front Range
  of the Rocky Mountains
- One W.I.N.–W.I.N. family night at each school
- Community leadership project service-learning activities

W.I.N.–W.I.N. is co-managed and financially supported by the Denver
Zoo and the Colorado Division of Wildlife, although day-to-day management of the program is the sole responsibility of the zoo. Beyond the zoo
and the Division of Wildlife, the Great Outdoors Colorado Trust Fund
(GOCO) has always provided substantial funding for the program. Its state
board is charged with disbursing expendable income from the Colorado lot-
tery to programs designed to help the people of Colorado preserve, enhance,
appreciate, and enjoy Colorado's parks, wildlife, trails, rivers, and open
space. Additional support for the program comes from W.I.N.–W.I.N.'s
thirty-nine partners, largely nonprofit organizations and governmental agencies with complementary foci and missions regarding the environment, conservation, and public education. A few of the partners serve primarily
advisory or training functions, but most provide on-site programming as
part of W.I.N.–W.I.N.'s field site visits. The partner site facilities available
for W.I.N.–W.I.N. use vary from wildlife refuges, parks, and farms to nature
centers, museums, and indoor aquariums.

The W.I.N.–W.I.N. program is an excellent illustration of the myriad relationships that can exist between nonformal education providers and their clients or audiences. At the broadest level, it illustrates a group of nonformal educational organizations (the Denver Zoo, the Colorado Division of Wildlife, and the thirty-nine partner sites) delivering educational services to a formal education client (twenty-five elementary schools in the metropolitan Denver area). The pre- and postvisit activities reflect formal instruction provided by classroom teachers in a traditional formal environment, and the in-class lessons are an example of nonformal educators' providing formal instruction in a formal classroom. The site visits represent formal instruction provided by nonformal educators in nonformal settings (the partner sites), and family night activities consist of nonformal educational opportunities occurring in a nonformal setting.

Using this complex and multifaceted program as a case study, the next section illustrates the various ways in which stakeholders can be involved in the development and implementation of an evaluation system in a setting that crosses formal and nonformal education boundaries.

## Getting to Know Each Other

When first approached by the zoo's director of education and volunteer services about the possibility of conducting an evaluation of the W.I.N.-W.I.N. program to determine its effectiveness, the evaluation team did what many other evaluators have to do. We explained that although we are open to a variety of approaches to evaluation, we preferred the more collaborative (O'Sullivan and D'Agostino, 2002) and participatory (Cousins and Whitmore, 1998) approaches to evaluation. Rather than conducting evaluations of programs, we preferred to facilitate stakeholder-based, utilization-focused (Patton, 1997) projects that did more than focus strictly on program outcomes. We went on to explain that since this approach to evaluation is based on working for and with specific, intended primary users for specific, intended uses, we would like to meet some of the key decision makers so that we could learn more about the program and provide them with information about us. Somewhat to our surprise, given all the realities of nonformal education providers discussed throughout this volume, we were invited to come to Denver for a few days. An even greater surprise was that the zoo offered to pay our way. Already we knew this was not an ordinary nonformal education provider.

During the subsequent exploratory visit, our involvement with program stakeholders was limited primarily to the individuals who were seeking and paying for the evaluation. As is usually the case, these people were the program managers and higher-level administrators from the two primary sponsoring organizations. Representatives from the zoo included the director of education and volunteer services, the zoo's W.I.N.–W.I.N. program manager, and the W.I.N.–W.I.N. program coordinator. The Division of Wildlife was represented by the acting chief of education and the Division's W.I.N.–W.I.N. program manager. Since part of the purpose of this initial meeting was to get to know as much as possible about the program in a short time, the W.I.N.–W.I.N. logistics coordinator and two W.I.N.–W.I.N. instructors participated in some of the activities as well.

Over the course of three days, we learned about the W.I.N.–W.I.N. program and its components through dialogue with the program administrators, brief discussions with program staff, visits to partner sites, and observations of the program in action. We also discussed the potential clients' desires related to evaluation, including why they felt evaluation was needed, how the evaluation was being funded, and what they hoped to get out of it. We covered all the usual matters addressed with potential clients.

In addition to learning about the program and its related personnel, another extremely important purpose of this visit was to let the potential clients get to know us. Before getting involved in what could be a very long relationship, we wanted to make sure the two teams were compatible. Besides providing basic information on our backgrounds and expertise, we spent substantial time presenting our beliefs about and approach to evaluation. We explained that based on a number of factors (time, money, and desire, among others), we liked to involve a variety of stakeholders in as many aspects of an evaluation as possible. We also summarized the benefits of doing so, such as the development of a shared understanding of the program, increased usability and use of results, and increased internal evaluation capacity, as well as some of the challenges, such as the substantial time commitment that would be needed.

## Examining the Program's Theory

By the end of the visit, we all felt we could work well together and decided our first step would be to conduct an evaluability assessment (Smith, 1989; Wholey, 1994) of the program to determine the type of evaluation for which the program was ready and that would be most beneficial. For this phase, the core team of decision makers (both W.I.N.–W.I.N. program managers, the W.I.N.–W.I.N. program coordinator, the W.I.N.–W.I.N. logistics coordinator, and the zoo's director of education and volunteer services) agreed to expand stakeholder involvement to include all of the program staff. Assuming all went well with each stage, we would proceed with designing an evaluation system for the program and incorporate additional stakeholders as appropriate as we went along.

The primary activity completed during the modified evaluability assessment was the construction of a logic model for W.I.N.–W.I.N. in order to examine its program theory. Over two months, using the Targeting Outcomes of Programs (TOP) model, also known as Bennett's hierarchy,

(Bennett and Rockwell, 2004), each component of the program was examined carefully to (1) clarify the primary and secondary audiences; (2) specify related inputs and outputs; (3) identify—often for the first time—the desired short-term, intermediate, and long-term outcomes; (4) indicate how these outcomes were connected to the program's stated mission; and (5) determine how the program components were (or in some cases, were not) connected to other components. The group also discussed major changes that had taken place since the program's inception and the reasons behind these changes. In addition, we reviewed the types and results of evaluation activities (both formal and informal) that had been incorporated into the program thus far, and we began exploring the types of information that would be useful to the program staff and administrators for future decision making. During this phase, the stakeholders often worked with the evaluators as a single group on tasks, but they were also divided into subgroups with duties that sometimes included work to be completed between visits from the evaluation team.

## Development of the Evaluation Plan

For the next step in the process, the development of an evaluation plan, stakeholder involvement was expanded once again. Working with the core team, we identified as many individuals and groups as possible who had a stake in the program and would be interested in the results of its evaluation. These groups were then divided into subgroups based on the extent to which their involvement was important or required (for process, informational, or political reasons) and the type of involvement that would be appropriate for that group's members. In this way, we began to distinguish between program stakeholders and evaluation stakeholders—those who would play an active role in the evaluation.

At this stage, we were looking to identify stakeholder groups that were most important to include and had the most to offer and gain from involvement in development of the evaluation plan. Although the list of program stakeholders was quite extensive, not all of them could be or would want to be involved in this process, and not everyone's involvement was necessary. For example, state legislators who enacted the Great Outdoors Colorado Trust Fund legislation, teachers and students from nonparticipating schools, and non-W.I.N.–W.I.N. education staff at the zoo all could be classified as program stakeholders who might well be interested in the current activities and outcomes resulting from it. However, it was agreed that each of these program stakeholder groups was too distant and disconnected from the program to warrant involvement in its evaluation.

Representatives from those stakeholder groups that were deemed accessible and most important to include in the process were brought together to form the W.I.N.–W.I.N. stakeholder advisory panel. Twenty-one individuals

## Table 3.1.  Members of the Stakeholder Advisory Panel

| Stakeholder | Advisory Panel Members |
| --- | --- |
| Primary program sponsors | Denver Zoo: Director of education and volunteer services |
| | Denver Zoo: Director of development |
| | Division of Wildlife: Acting director of education |
| Program managers | W.I.N.–W.I.N. program manager stationed at the Denver Zoo |
| | W.I.N.–W.I.N. program manager stationed at the DOW |
| | W.I.N.–W.I.N. program coordinator |
| | W.I.N.–W.I.N. logistics coordinator |
| Program providers | W.I.N.–W.I.N. instructors (3) |
| | Other W.I.N.–W.I.N. staff (2) |
| | W.I.N.–W.I.N. partner sites (3) |
| Program participants | Principals (2) |
| | Teachers (2) |
| | Family members (1) |
| Other | Colorado Department of Education (1) |

*Note:* This table is meant to represent several layers of stakeholder participation: (1) the broad stakeholder groups who participated on the Stakeholder Advisory Panel (program sponsors, program managers, program providers, and program participants); (2) the subgroups of stakeholders within these broader stakeholder groups; and (3) the number of each of the subgroups that participated.

representing multiple stakeholder groups, as outlined in Table 3.1, agreed to participate. There were additional individuals and groups from whom information was needed for this phase but either could not, chose not, or were not appropriate to participate on the advisory panel. For example, the advisory panel agreed that communication about the evaluation should be maintained with top-level administrators from the primary program sponsors. Rather than serve on the panel, however, representatives from Great Outdoors Colorado Trust Fund and the Denver Zoo Trustees asked to be kept informed by occasionally checking in with them through verbal or written updates. Students, another very important stakeholder group from whom input was needed, required yet a different approach.

Given the ages of the student audience (preschool to fifth grade) and the nature of the activities the advisory panel was undertaking, it was not appropriate to involve students intensively in the process of developing the evaluation plan. While various stakeholders felt they understood the student perspective fairly well and agreed to do their best to represent them, the advisory panel also wanted to get some sort of direct input from the group. Therefore, two members of the evaluation team and the W.I.N.–W.I.N. program coordinator conducted a discussion group with fourteen students from one representative school to identify a set of evaluation questions from the student perspective.

The stakeholder advisory panel held four half-day meetings, with "homework" in between, during which information gathered from the students and other absent stakeholders was incorporated into an assortment of activities. While it is important to note that final approval always rested with members of the core team, this group of stakeholders undertook a variety of tasks to provide detailed advice and recommendations on virtually all aspects of the evaluation plan. Over the course of four months, the panel engaged in the following tasks and activities:

- Participated in Evaluation 101, a brief introduction to and overview of evaluation
- Reviewed stakeholder representatives to determine if any critical perspective was missing
- Discussed needs and desires regarding evaluation of the program
- Developed a set of evaluation questions
- Reviewed and grouped the questions
- Prioritized and eliminated inappropriate and unfeasible questions
- Discussed preferences and need for types of information and data (qualitative and quantitative)
- Identified data sources and type of data collection instruments appropriate to gather information needed to address each question
- Prioritized data sources and type of data collection instruments based on available time and money
- Developed a time line for administration
- Discussed preferences for presentation of results
- Discussed ideas for disseminating results to primary stakeholders and a broader audience
- Periodically reviewed progress to date, answered questions, and addressed issues as needed

Before and after each advisory panel meeting, the evaluation team also independently met with the core team to review the project's progress and results up to that point. In addition, we often discussed the core team's feelings about how the project was progressing and the effects it was having on the program, themselves, and other program staff. This ensured that decision-making authority continued to lie in the hands of the core team and did not get lost in the activity and intensity of the stakeholder meetings. It also contributed to the ongoing growth of these team members by giving them an opportunity to regularly reflect on the process, get answers to any questions they had about it, and expand their ability to think evaluatively (Patton, 2002). As King (1998) emphasizes, although these types of discussions are time-consuming, they are critical for participants to create shared meanings of their experiences. The more the group shares joint own-ership in the program and its evaluation, the more likely it is that they will find it interesting and work together to solve problems and move ahead.

At the end of the four-month period, the group had produced a model plan (see Norland, Heimlich, and Somers, 2000) for an evaluation system that, if implemented in its entirety, would provide information for (1) immediate, short-term program improvement at the activity level (Com-ponent 1); (2) correlational-level indicators of program outcomes and monitoring over time for long-term program improvement and develop-ment (Component 2); and (3) the establishment of student outcomes based on experimental and quasi-experimental studies (Component 3). Based on a number of factors, including time, money, and the immediate needs of the program sponsors, the core team selected fourteen instruments and data-gathering techniques from components 1 and 2 to conduct a pilot test of the evaluation system. The pilot test of these instruments also served as an implementation evaluation of the program as it was being delivered at that time.

## Instrument Development

During the instrument development phase of most evaluations, stakeholder involvement reduces substantially or ceases altogether. Often a select group of stakeholders will review and approve draft forms and procedures, but rarely any more than that. After all, evaluators usually are brought in to "conduct" evaluation. Clients sometimes (perhaps even often) believe the creation and implementation of data collection tools is what evaluation is all about and what professional evaluators do best. It is rare for stakehold-ers to have any training or background in instrument design and construc-tion, and although stakeholders normally experience some level of anxiety about participating in or receiving the results of an evaluation (Donaldson, Gooler, and Scriven, 2002), they may view the instrument development stage as particularly mysterious, confusing, or perhaps even frightening. Thus they, and sometimes the evaluators as well, feel this process is best left to the "experts."

However, in order to ask questions that are really meaningful and gather data that will be useful, stakeholder input is very important in this phase of evaluation. Based on our experiences with the stakeholder advi-sory panel thus far, we realized this group was capable of assisting with this process. More important, all but one panel member wanted to continue working on the project and be part of bringing the evaluation plan to life. So rather than reduce stakeholder involvement at this point, the size of the advisory panel actually increased to twenty-eight as three new partner rep-resentatives, four more teachers, and the four remaining instructors joined the group.

As with the earlier panel, the Phase II stakeholder advisory panel made recommendations on virtually every aspect of this phase of the project, but everything was taken to the core team for final approval. It should be noted, however, that there was not a single instance when the core team pulled rank to override a proposal made by the panel. There were a few times that the panel referred decisions to the core team rather than take a position on an issue, usually on issues related to the amount of funding that should be made available for a particular activity or component.

During the instrument development phase, the advisory panel regularly met as a full group to discuss cross-cutting issues and tasks. In addition, the panel divided into subgroups based on their familiarity with and interest in different data sources and instruments (core team, student, teacher, instructor, partner, and principal). These six work groups met routinely over a five-month period and, under the guidance of the evaluation team, transformed the stakeholder evaluation questions into instrument questions, checklists, and discussion points for each of fourteen different data collection methods and two developmental activities. Based on this extensive input from the work groups, the evaluation team designed and formatted the questionnaires, feedback forms, observation forms, interview schedules, and focus group discussion guides. Each work group then revised and refined its respective instruments, and, finally, the full advisory panel reviewed the entire set before they were pilot-tested.

## Pilot Test: Administration, Analysis, and Interpretation of the Evaluation Instruments

Most of the stakeholder advisory panel took a break from the evaluation during the data collection phase of the evaluation. However, a number of stakeholders, the program staff in particular, remained quite busy and involved over this period.

W.I.N.–W.I.N. management was responsible for the following activities:

• Selecting the random sample of classes
• Mailing advance notice letters to the principals of each W.I.N.–W.I.N. school
• Mailing forms to each partner site and collecting completed forms
• Monitoring completion of all forms and checking on nonrespondents
• Conducting interviews with the principal of each W.I.N.–W.I.N. school
• Identifying and recruiting participants for the teacher and student focus groups and arranging for the facilities and refreshments for each gathering
• Overseeing activities assigned to the instructors

Instructors were responsible for the following activities:

- Delivering advance notice letters to the teachers of the selected classrooms and personally obtaining the commitment of each of these teachers to participate in the evaluation
- Assisting with the compilation of instrument packets for all questionnaires
- Delivering forms to each school and picking up completed forms from each school
- Implementing one developmental activity (instructor discussion groups) and completing two instruments (classroom observation sheet and instructor questionnaire)
- Distributing and collecting two instruments (parent questionnaire and family night feedback form) during family night at each school
- Entering data from completed family night feedback forms into Microsoft Word (including translating data from Spanish to English as necessary)
- Entering student questionnaire data from the classes they instructed into SPSS (including translating data from Spanish into English as necessary)

In addition, two stakeholders were trained to serve as the assistant moderators for some of the focus groups. A previous W.I.N.–W.I.N. instructor helped moderate the teacher focus groups, and the W.I.N.–W.I.N. program coordinator served as the assistant for the student focus groups.

## Interpretation of Results and Next Steps

After all pilot data had been collected, entered, and initially analyzed, the six work groups met separately one more time. At these meetings, the groups reviewed preliminary analyses of both quantitative and qualitative data from the instruments they helped design, explored how data from within and across instruments were related, discussed implications of the findings, selected items to be included in the final presentation, and suggested additional analyses. In addition, each group discussed the successes and challenges that occurred during the administration of the instruments and made suggestions for revisions in the instruments and future implementation.

The involvement of stakeholders was brought full circle at the final meeting of the advisory panel. Rather than a simple presentation of the pilot results, the final meeting was an active dialogue about the implications of the initial findings for the W.I.N.–W.I.N. program, the stakeholder group they represented, and themselves as individuals. Based on this discussion, the panel created action plans to address issues identified through the evaluation process, reviewed changes that had already occurred in the program, and discussed time lines for additional changes and future implementation of the evaluation system. The group also discussed reactions to the evaluation from both a personal and professional perspective.

## So, Did It Work? A Look Back at the Results

Our reasoning and justification for involving so many stakeholders so intensely in the evaluation process were based on the assumption that the benefits would outweigh the costs of doing so. The primary benefits we touted to the clients were the development of a shared understanding of the program, resulting in increased buy-in and ownership, increased usability and use of evaluation findings, and increased internal evaluation capacity. So, did our assumptions hold true? Did the benefits materialize, and did they outweigh the costs? To find the answers to these questions, we look at the changes and outcomes we witnessed throughout the evaluation process.

The value of involving a variety of stakeholders with multiple points of view was evident early in the process. For example, creation of the logic models and explication of W.I.N.–W.I.N.'s program theory could have been accomplished in a number of ways and did not necessarily require the direct involvement of any stakeholders. However, including program administrators as well as all of the program staff in this phase produced a number of positive results. Based on check-in activities we conducted throughout the project, it was clear that all staff members developed a much more detailed, in-depth understanding of the program, including its history and the intentions of original program designers as well as how the program was currently being implemented. In addition, the forum and format of the evaluability assessment meetings and activities fostered extensive information exchange between program administrators and program staff, with both groups gaining a greater understanding and appreciation of the other's point of view. Staff learned more about funding and other concerns faced by the administration, and administrators learned more about the constraints as well as the joys experienced by the staff in their day-to-day interaction with students, teachers, and parents.

The shared understanding of the program developed through this process allowed staff members to look at each activity in a new light. With an expanded awareness of the program's history, they came to appreciate how politics and other influences had affected the design of the program and why certain activities existed in their current form. As a group, they came to realize that some activities were not designed to address W.I.N.–W.I.N.'s goals but rather existed for other, perhaps completely unrelated, reasons. Based on their day-to-day interaction with the structure and function of the program, they then were able to begin examining each component, determine how well it fit within the logic model, and, if necessary, generate ideas for changes that would make it better aligned with program goals. For example, when the group came to the realization that families were a secondary rather than a primary audience for the program, the structure and function of the family-related activities changed substantially. The focus of

NEW DIRECTIONS FOR EVALUATION • DOI 10.1002/ev

these activities became more centered on reinforcing student learning and less on educating parents and siblings.

The types of dialogue and discussion used during the evaluability assessment and throughout the evaluation afforded participants, especially program staff and members of the core team, time to think about the program. As other facilitators of collaborative evaluations have found (for example, Torres and others, 2000), these opportunities for reflection and sense making are highly valued by participants. At various points over the twenty-month project, nearly all stakeholders commented on how much they appreciated being given the time to reflect on what this program was meant to be, the role they and their organization played in it, and what they really wanted to accomplish through their involvement with it. They recognized that the evaluation process had forced them to step away from their day-to-day duties to look at the big picture; not only were they grateful for that opportunity, but they also found it meaningful and valuable.

Regarding use of the findings, the W.I.N.–W.I.N. program has used information from the evaluation in a number of ways. In the months following completion of the pilot test, W.I.N.–W.I.N. staff and other stakeholders presented findings from the pilot evaluation to various audiences including other zoo staff, Division of Wildlife administrators, all partner organizations, and representatives from Great Outdoors Colorado Trust Fund, as well as at a number of regional and national conferences. Immediate changes to the program included developing a customized computer software program to streamline and simplify scheduling and hiring a language acquisition specialist to present a workshop for partner sites that did not have bilingual staff. Longer-term action plans developed at the end of the pilot evaluation included experimenting with different approaches for increasing parental access and connection to the program's partner organizations, improving and expanding training for teachers, and the creation of a quarterly newsletter. Since the 2000–2001 pilot test, W.I.N.–W.I.N. management and staff have continued to implement the evaluation instruments and make changes to the program based on the information they gather. As this chapter is being written, they are in the process of contracting with a consultant to assist them with a longitudinal examination of the data they have collected over the past four years.

In addition to guiding program improvements, data from the evaluation have been integrated into the program's marketing and promotional materials. For example, an informational booklet was developed based on the evaluation and distributed to all participating schools and partners as well as any other interested parties (see Somers, 2002). This booklet is used to introduce the program to new principals, teachers, and others with an interest in the program. It has also been helpful to various schools, partners, and the W.I.N.–W.I.N. program itself in providing justification for continued funding and participation in the program.

Our third primary reason for a high level of stakeholder involvement was to build evaluation capacity. Although increasing evaluation capacity is sometimes considered a bonus or secondary outcome of a participatory approach, some evaluators believe it should be an explicit aim of the process (Burke, 1998), and it was a highly intentional goal of this evaluation. We were interested in directly benefiting the individuals involved, and, through them, we hoped to benefit the larger environmental education community.

Evidence of increased capacity became apparent early in the process and continues today. For example, even while we were in the middle of developing the program theory for each W.I.N.–W.I.N. component, members of the program staff began working with other staff at the zoo to employ logic modeling techniques in the design of new education programs. One of these, the Young Scientists program, not only used logic modeling to develop the program but conducted an implementation evaluation during the program's second year to make sure the program was being implemented as designed and to look for areas of improvement before getting too focused on program outcomes. Young Scientists since has become the zoo's most successful and highly rated program for middle-school students with twelve hundred participants from fifteen schools currently enrolled.

Stakeholders also shared their new knowledge and skills with audiences beyond the zoo. For example, two staff members presented the W.I.N.–W.I.N. program theory and the process used to develop it at a national science education conference in San Francisco, and one of the partners gave a presentation on the program's evaluation at a national conference for museum educators. In one presentation (to the International Association of Avian Trainers and Educators), the stakeholder went beyond the W.I.N.–W.I.N. evaluation to focus on the overall importance of evaluation and led the group in a discussion of possible ways to evaluate wildlife shows.

One organization beyond the Denver Zoo that was substantially affected by participation in the evaluation was the Colorado Division of Wildlife. The primary stakeholder from the division has indicated that since participating in the evaluation, she has used the Targeting Program Outcomes model (Bennett and Rockwell, 2004) in all subsequent programs or projects to which she was assigned (W. Hanophy, personal communication to the author, November 15, 2004). Furthermore, the evaluation and model were shared with other division education staff statewide, and many now use some type of preliminary evaluation or program development techniques at the start of new projects.

The result of all of these stakeholder-led activities is that evaluation knowledge and techniques were shared with numerous individuals far beyond the W.I.N.–W.I.N. program itself. One of the most exciting aspects of these activities was that they were undertaken without prompting from the evaluation team. Based solely on the clients' experiences, growth in understanding, and perception of value of the evaluation process, they felt it was worth sharing and teaching to others.

## Advocating for Participatory Evaluation in Nonformal Education Settings

Many factors must be considered when determining the precise approach that will be taken in any specific evaluation. The distinctive context and individuals involved in each program inevitably mean that every evaluation will be different, so no single approach to evaluation should be considered a "one size fits all" methodology. There are, of course, circumstances in which limited stakeholder involvement is appropriate. However, I will argue that there are certain characteristics about nonformal education settings and nonformal educators that call for using a participatory approach to evaluation whenever possible.

One reason participatory evaluation is particularly well suited to these settings is that it fits the philosophy and approach to education promoted by nonformal educators. The philosophical and practical approach to education advanced by the literature on nonformal education methodology focuses substantial attention on the direct involvement of learners in the development and execution of their own educational experiences (North American Association for Environmental Education, 1999, 2004). This constructivist approach to education recognizes that individuals begin, participate in, and end programs with different understandings of the subject matter based on their personal backgrounds and previous experiences. In addition, this approach emphasizes that the more personally relevant an educational experience is, the more likely it is that the learners will incorporate the experience into their lives in a lasting and meaningful way. This echoes the reasons for stakeholder involvement put forth by those who advocate inclusive approaches to evaluation (see Cousins and Earl, 1992; Fetterman, 2001; and Ryan and others, 1998). Just as participants learn from being personally engaged in nonformal settings, stakeholders learn from their engagement in the evaluation process.

The need to increase evaluation capacity is another reason nonformal educators and administrators should embrace participatory approaches to evaluation. As suggested in Chapters One, Four, and Five of this volume and elsewhere, the occurrence of in-depth, high-quality program evaluation in nonformal education settings, and in environmental education settings in particular, is very low. Individuals employed in these settings who possess evaluation-related knowledge and skills are even rarer. The need for increased evaluation capacity is tremendous. As demonstrated in this case study, collaborative, participatory, stakeholder-based evaluation is an important means by which evaluation knowledge can be increased.

A third argument for high levels of stakeholder involvement is that it allows clients to accomplish more with less money. While the evaluation described in this chapter was expensive compared to many nonformal education evaluations (total cost was approximately $150,000—10 percent of one year's overall program costs and roughly 20 percent of direct annual funding), we could not have done as much as we did without the intensive involvement of stakeholders throughout the process. Admittedly, there are a number of items that took more of the evaluators' time than would be necessary in a less interactive evaluation approach, and the evaluator's hourly pay is often one of the highest direct costs of an evaluation. For example, it is time- and energy-consuming to track and maintain communication with stakeholders, facilitate frequent stakeholder meetings, and develop materials for training and stakeholder involvement. However, there were numerous contributions and duties undertaken by the stakeholders that would have greatly increased direct costs if they were assumed by the evaluation team and charged to the client. Examples of cost-saving activities carried out by W.I.N.–W.I.N. management and staff included oversight of all instrument distribution and collection, direct data collection activities (including conducting interviews and acting as assistant focus group moderators), and data entry of information from the majority of the instruments.

Participatory evaluation is also a cost-effective means for increasing internal evaluation capacity. Unlike a generic training program that providers might take part in elsewhere, the evaluation knowledge and skills taught in a collaborative evaluation are directly applicable to the participants' ongoing job responsibilities. This type of personally focused, situation-specific training would be difficult and quite expensive to obtain through university courses, attending conferences and workshops, or contracting with a consultant. Therefore, when the evaluation knowledge and skills of program staff and other stakeholders are improved through participation in a collaborative evaluation, the value of dollars spent can extend far beyond a particular evaluation and lead to improved planning and decision making at the organizational level.

## Conclusion

As illustrated throughout this chapter, extensive stakeholder involvement in the development and implementation of evaluation can result in extensive changes not only to the program being evaluated but to the individuals and organizations involved as well. These changes in thinking, skills, and behavior—what Patton (1997) refers to as process use—move the outcomes of an evaluation far beyond the changes that might occur based on the findings alone. Given the match in philosophy, the need for increased evaluation understanding and capacity, and the economic value that participatory evaluation can represent for organizations (especially nonprofits), nonformal educators should carefully consider how and to what extent they can involve stakeholders in their next evaluation endeavor.

## References

Bennett, C., and Rockwell, K. "Targeting Outcomes of Programs: TOP." 2004. http://cit-news.unl.edu/TOP/english/index.html.

Bentrup, G. "Evaluation of a Collaborative Model: A Case Study Analysis of Watershed Planning in the Intermountain West." *Environmental Management,* 2001, 27(5), 739–748.

Blahna, D., and Yonts-Shepard, S. "Public Involvement in Resource Planning: Toward Bridging the Gap Between Policy and Implementation." *Society and Natural Resources,* 1989, 2(3), 209–227.

Burke, B. "Evaluating for a Change: Reflections on Participatory Methodology." In E. Whitmore (ed.), *Understanding and Practicing Participatory Evaluation.* New Directions for Evaluation, no. 80. San Francisco: Jossey-Bass, 1998.

Committee on Audience Research and Evaluation. *Introduction to Museum Evaluation.* Washington, D.C.: American Association of Museums, 1997.

Cousins, J. B., and Earl, L. M. "The Case for Participatory Evaluation." *Educational Evaluation and Policy Analysis,* 1992, 14(4), 397–418.

Cousins, J. B., and Whitmore, E. "Framing Participatory Evaluation." In E. Whitmore (ed.), *Understanding and Practicing Participatory Evaluation.* New Directions for Evaluation, no. 80. San Francisco: Jossey-Bass, 1998.

Denver Zoological Foundation. "The Wonders in Nature–Wonders in Neighborhoods (W.I.N.–W.I.N.) Program." 2000. http://www.denverzoo.org/education/school_programs/outreach/win_win/win_win.htm.

Diamond, J. *Practical Evaluation Guide: Tools for Museums and Other Informal Educational Settings.* Walnut Creek, Calif.: AltaMira Press, 1999.

Donaldson, S. I., Gooler, L. E., and Scriven, M. "Strategies for Managing Evaluation Anxiety: Toward a Psychology of Program Evaluation." *American Journal of Evaluation,* 2002, 23(3), 261–273.

Fetterman, D. M. *Foundations of Empowerment Evaluation.* Thousand Oaks, Calif.: Sage, 2001.

Frechtling, J. (ed.). *Footprints: Strategies for Non-Traditional Program Evaluation.* Arlington, Va.: National Science Foundation, 1995.

Frechtling, J. *The 2002 User-Friendly Handbook for Project Evaluation.* Arlington, Va.: National Science Foundation, 2002.

King, J. A. "Making Sense of Participatory Evaluation Practice." In E. Whitmore (ed.), *Understanding and Practicing Participatory Evaluation.* New Directions for Evaluation, no. 80. San Francisco: Jossey-Bass, 1998.

McCurley, S., and Vineyard, S. *Measuring Up: Assessment Tools for Volunteer Programs.* Darien, Ill.: Heritage Arts Publishing, 2003.

McDuff, M. "Needs Assessment for Participatory Evaluation of Environmental Education Programs." *Applied Environmental Education and Communication,* 2002, 1, 25–36.

Norland, E., Heimlich, J. E., and Somers, C. "Evaluation Plan for Wonders in Nature–Wonders in Neighborhoods." Unpublished report. Denver: W.I.N.–W.I.N. Stakeholder Advisory Panel for the Colorado Division of Wildlife and the Denver Zoological Society, 2000.

North American Association for Environmental Education. *Excellence in Environmental Education: Guidelines for Learning (K-12).* Washington, D.C.: North American Association for Environmental Education, 1999.

North American Association for Environmental Education. *Nonformal Environmental Education Programs: Guidelines for Excellence.* Washington, D.C.: North American Association for Environmental Education, 2004.

O'Sullivan, R., and D'Agostino, A. "Promoting Evaluation Through Collaboration." *Evaluation,* 2002, *8*(3), 372–387.

Patton, M. Q. *Utilization-Focused Evaluation.* (3rd ed.) Thousand Oaks, Calif.: Sage, 1997.

Patton, M. Q. "A Vision of Evaluation That Strengthens Democracy." *Evaluation,* 2002, *8*(1), 125–139.

Ryan, K. E., and others. "Advantages and Challenges of Using Inclusive Approaches in Evaluation Practice." *American Journal of Evaluation,* 1998, *19*(1), 101–122.

Selin, S., and Chavez, D. "Developing a Collaborative Model for Environmental Planning and Management." *Environmental Management,* 1995, *19*(2), 189–195.

Smith, M. F. *Evaluability Assessment: A Practical Approach.* Norwell, Mass.: Kluwer, 1989.

Somers, C. *Wonders in Nature–Wonders in Neighborhoods: Bringing Together the Worlds of Wildlife and Children.* Denver: W.I.N.–W.I.N. Managing Partners, Colorado Division of Wildlife and Denver Zoological Society, 2002.

Thomson, G., and Hoffman, J. "Measuring the Success of Environmental Education Programs." Canadian Parks and Wilderness Society, 2004. http://www.cpawscalgary.org/education/evaluation.

Torres, R. T., and others. "Dialogue and Reflection in a Collaborative Evaluation: Stakeholder and Evaluator Voices." In K. E. Ryan and L. DeStafano (eds.), *Evaluation as a Democratic Process: Promoting Inclusion, Dialogue, and Deliberation.* New Directions for Evaluation, no. 85. San Francisco: Jossey-Bass, 2000.

Whitmore, E. (ed.). *Understanding and Practicing Participatory Evaluation.* New Directions for Evaluation, no. 80. San Francisco: Jossey-Bass, 1998.

Wholey, J. S. "Assessing the Feasibility and Likely Usefulness of Evaluation." In J. S. Wholey, H. P. Hatry, and K. E. Newcomer (eds.), *Handbook of Practical Program Evaluation.* San Francisco: Jossey-Bass, 1994.

Wondolleck, J., and Yaffee, S. *Making Collaboration Work: Lessons from Innovation in Natural Resource Management.* Covelo, Calif.: Island Press, 2000.

*CINDY SOMERS is an evaluation and program development consultant working in Denver, Colorado.*

4

*This chapter describes some of the challenges presented by nonformal education settings and discusses strategies for increasing evaluation use in nonformal education programs.*

# Evaluation Use in Nonformal Education Settings

*Kate Clavijo, M. Lynette Fleming, Elizabeth F. Hoermann, Stacie A. Toal, Kelli Johnson*

Decision makers in nonformal education programs can maximize the utility of their evaluation investment and improve program effectiveness by being more mindful of the potential uses of evaluation information. Evaluation use is a multifaceted construct that may include, but is not limited to, the implementation of evaluation recommendations or results. Three primary types of evaluation use have emerged from four decades of scholarly research: (1) instrumental, where the results are used in making decisions about program structure and function; (2) conceptual, where the results inform or educate decision makers about matters related to the program or topic being evaluated; and (3) persuasive or symbolic, where the results are used to influence or persuade others. This chapter expands on these definitions of evaluation use, describes some of the challenges presented by nonformal education settings, and discusses strategies for increasing evaluation use in nonformal education programs.

## Evaluation Use Defined

In the past few years, some researchers have sought to expand the concept of evaluation use to a broader construct called evaluation *influence*, which encompasses changes both within and outside the evaluation context, during the evaluation and immediately or at any time following the evaluation (Kirkhart, 2000; Mark and Henry, 2004). These researchers argue that we

New Directions for Evaluation, no. 108, Winter 2005   © Wiley Periodicals, Inc.
Published online in Wiley InterScience (www.interscience.wiley.com) • DOI: 10.1002/ev.170

should be more interested in the overall impact of the evaluation rather than strictly in the use of its results or process. This broader category of influence captures all of the consequences of an evaluation, including ones that are not limited by time and context (Henry and Mark, 2003; Kirkhart, 2000). To accommodate the complexities of this construct, Kirkhart (2000) proposes three dimensions of influence: sources, intentions, and time. For program directors, this broad concept may better capture the far-reaching effects of an evaluation on different stakeholders in both the short and long terms.

While research on influence may ultimately prove useful to the field, evaluators in nonformal education settings can immediately benefit from understanding earlier research on use. The most logical and understandable use of evaluation results, where evaluation findings have a direct impact on decision making, is labeled *instrumental*. For example, an evaluation by Maryland's Chesapeake Bay Foundation found that providing environmental education curriculum combined with field experiences for students was more effective in deepening the respect students felt toward outdoor settings than curriculum and professional development alone. The foundation used these evaluation results to shape its program offerings to schools, resulting in the creation of two additional programs offering field experiences to students and teachers (Zint, Kraemer, Northway, and Miyoun, 2002).

Evaluation findings do not always have such a direct impact on decision making. Instead, evaluation results may shape the decision maker's thinking, ideas, or opinions without resulting in any action directly attributable to the evaluation. This type of evaluation use is referred to as *conceptual* use. As Rossi, Freeman, and Lipsey (1999) describe it, "The conceptual use of evaluation results creeps into the policy and program worlds by a variety of routes, usually circuitous, that are difficult to trace" (p. 446). While program directors may be unlikely to change current programs to accommodate all evaluation findings, the results taken as a whole may affect their perspectives or help them think differently about their programs. Thus, conceptual uses result not in specific actions, but rather in a change of thinking or attitude. For example, a Minnesota skilled nursing facility recently conducted an evaluation of its interprofessional health care team. Prior to the evaluation, the administrator was not favorably inclined toward the interprofessional care delivery model. However, the evaluation results demonstrated a positive impact on certain aspects of the quality of care. As a result, the administrator changed his view of the program and was much more accepting of it and its personnel.

The third general type of use, *symbolic* or *persuasive* use, occurs when an evaluation is used to validate or legitimize a program rather than gain a true picture of its merit or worth. Alkin and Taut (2003) summarize the context and reason that symbolic use occurs as "situations where evaluation was used to either justify a decision that had been previously made or to demonstrate that a program was willing to be evaluated, thus enhancing the reputation of the program manager or decision-maker" (p. 5). This type of evaluation use is also known as *political* use and is typically considered in a negative light (Greene, 1988; Huie Hofstetter and Alkin, 2003; Torres and Preskill, 2001; Weiss, Murphey-Graham, and Birkeland, 2005). For example, a public health education and outreach effort to provide street-side HIV prevention education to at-risk youth came under political fire in a recent election year. Because of what it termed the "obscene nature" of the program's promotional materials, which contained photographs with sexual (specifically homosexual) overtones, an influential lobby group protested state funding. In response, legislators threatened to eliminate state funding for the program unless the program was evaluated. In response, the program director immediately began an evaluation of the program, and funding was secured even before the evaluation was completed. It was primarily the willingness to evaluate, not the actual impact of the program or results of the evaluation, that convinced the legislators to continue funding for the program.

Instrumental, conceptual, and symbolic use focus exclusively on how evaluation results are used. However, a growing body of evaluation research contends that this focus on results should be expanded to include a consideration of the impact of participation in the evaluation process as well. Patton (1997) describes this category of evaluation use, *process use,* as the changes in personal, programmatic, or organizational thinking and behavior as a result of going through an evaluation. Alkin and Taut (2003) add that the process of evaluation may also help stakeholders acquire new information or learn new skills. Forss, Rebien, and Carlsson (2002) have suggested five types of process use: learning to learn, developing professional networks, creating shared understandings, strengthening the project, and boosting morale.

For example, an evaluation of the youth and family alcohol and drug prevention education program in a rural state found no significant results of the effectiveness of this program in keeping young people away from alcohol, tobacco, and other drugs. However, project staff reported having developed new perspectives on their curriculum after interacting with the program evaluators. As a result, they changed the way they collected information about the students' experiences, so that new data could be used in future evaluations. Although the findings of the evaluation may not have been the desired ones, the participants learned the value of thorough data collection during the evaluation.

## Challenges to Evaluation Use in Nonformal Education

Nonformal education encompasses a broad range of educational settings and methods outside the traditional, formal, structured classroom. Researchers have described nonformal education as more learner-centered, focused on the present, responsive to localized needs, and less structured. In addition, there is often a nonhierarchical relationship between learner and facilitator (Taylor and Calderelli, 2004). These characteristics pose unique challenges to using the results of evaluations in nonformal educational settings. The following observations and insights are based on our experiences with nonformal educational evaluations. Although these factors sometimes crop up within the formal educational system, we would argue that the challenges to evaluation use are more intensely present in nonformal educational settings and cluster in the areas of system infrastructure, scheduling, staffing, and financing:

• *Observation One: Many nonformal education settings lack an established infrastructure for understanding and interpreting evaluation results and therefore require catch-up work before evaluation results can be effectively used.*

Few nonformal educational settings boast formal testing, assessment, or evaluation structures, while school systems have used testing and program evaluation for decades. Most school districts have research and planning offices that use evaluation to assist officials in making programmatic decisions. Furthermore, with passage of the federal No Child Left Behind Act, schools and teachers are held increasingly accountable to local, state, and federal laws. Although there is disagreement as to the effectiveness of these measures, the very existence of a common measurement infrastructure distinguishes formal from nonformal education.

In practice, evaluations of nonformal organizations are interjected into environments where there is often little understanding of evaluation practice and use and little shared meaning relative to evaluation results. Thus, the nonformal education settings must frequently invest in creating shared meaning and building understanding of evaluation outcomes. This lack of existing infrastructure and standardization requires additional work by nonformal programs to create a foundation on which to build potential use of evaluation results.

• *Observation Two: Nonformal settings typically provide educational programming on intermittent or seasonal schedules with temporary or transient staff, which creates a barrier to effective use of evaluation results.*

Nonformal programs may be less likely to use evaluation results in an instrumental way, that is, to implement programmatic changes, because the seasonal or intermittent nature of these programs may hinder effective follow-up due to extended gaps between course offerings. In addition, the personnel involved in nonformal education settings are typically more transient than those in formal, or school-based, education settings. Unlike school teachers, staff in nonformal settings often are supported through grants, seasonal funds, and other nonpermanent funding sources, sometimes for as little as two or three months. Consequently, the staff responsible for implementing programmatic changes may not have participated in the evaluation or originally felt the need for change, and evaluators may hear clients say something like, "We can't use those evaluation results. That was her evaluation, and she left two months ago." As Patton (1997) suggests, the staff's dedication to the evaluation project has a strong influence over whether the results of that evaluation will be used. Thus, staff instability in nonformal settings may be a barrier to evaluation use, because the buy-in generated from having initiated and participated in the evaluation process is difficult to maintain due to staff transience.

• *Observation Three: Dependence on external funding is more pronounced among nonformal educational organizations, leading to a preponderance of symbolic or persuasive evaluation use.*

Although formal education providers sometimes rely on external funding, evaluation teams in these settings are more likely to use evaluation data to improve the organization and build expertise for future programs (Mark, Henry, and Julnes, 2000). On the other hand, a large percentage of nonformal education providers rely on external, and often project-by-project, government- or foundation-provided grant funding. Thus, when used, evaluation results in these settings are often directed at satisfying benefactors or securing additional funding—persuasive uses of the data. Program improvement may be a secondary goal of the evaluation team, or it may be completely overlooked in the search for money to provide more programming.

## Strategies for Facilitating Evaluation Use in Nonformal Education

Decision makers frequently limit their concern to how the results of an evaluation can be used persuasively or perhaps instrumentally. However, given the challenges related to evaluation use in nonformal settings, they would be well served to broaden their thinking to include conceptual and process uses as well. When evaluators and practitioners work to create a culture of evaluation with a commitment to evaluation use (regardless of use type), they appreciably increase the likelihood that the evaluation can result in organizational learning or improvement. We believe that decision makers in nonformal education settings can maximize the effectiveness of their evaluation efforts if they adopt the following strategies related to the type of person selected to conduct the evaluation, the process employed in conducting the evaluation, and the actions they take based on the results of the evaluation.

**Evaluator Screening and Selection.** Because there is often no designated evaluation department in nonformal settings, the evaluator is more likely to play a prominent role in implementing all phases of the evaluation. Therefore, careful selection of an evaluator appropriate for the organization is a critical first step. It is especially important that decision makers in a nonformal organization are mindful of whether there is a match between the philosophies of the program and the evaluator.

Given the incredible diversity of nonformal sites and programs, an evaluator who is sensitive to the subtleties of an individual program or setting will be better able to guide the process and provide a measure of continuity that would otherwise be lost given the often transient nature of programs and personnel in nonformal settings. It stands to reason that when the evaluator is attentive to the unique characteristics of the program and incorporates these into the evaluation, the evaluation will be more reflective of the people who will eventually be using the results. Patton (1997) asserts that evaluations conducted in light of this "personal factor" will increase the chances that the resulting evaluation will not just sit on a shelf.

The selection of a suitable evaluator can also increase the likelihood of conceptual evaluation use because an evaluator who is in tune with the organization will be more likely to create an evaluation environment in which people can remain open-minded. And, finally, while the results may be used in a persuasive fashion to secure support or funding, an evaluation conducted solely for these purposes ignores one fundamental purpose of evaluation: to judge the merit or worth of a program. Without such honest judgment and potential recommendations for improvement, the program may not maximize its evaluation investment.

Recently the Howard County Conservancy in Woodstock, Maryland, had an opportunity to hire an evaluator whose approach to evaluation mirrored its approach to education. The Howard County Conservancy runs education programs to provide residents with opportunities to learn about nature and the environment through programs and classes, restoration projects and demonstrations, and service-learning opportunities. The conservancy's educational programs follow the constructivist learning model and encourage children to become engaged, explore, and explain what they observe. In keeping with that philosophy, they hired an evaluator to conduct a formative evaluation, using direct input from program staff in a manner that mirrored the constructivist learning model. Staff were encouraged to get involved, question, and discuss all aspects of the evaluation. This strategy helped staff learn about the evaluation effort and how to use the evaluation results.

**Evaluation Process and Participation.** An evaluator with program knowledge and a commitment to the personal factor will ideally lead an evaluation process that includes many people across the organization. By virtue of this increased participation, the evaluation results will reach more people. Although many participants will not have the positional authority to use the evaluation instrumentally, their involvement makes it possible for them to use the evaluation in a conceptual manner, affirming or potentially changing their perspectives. In addition, the broad involvement of project personnel at all stages of the evaluation is likely to create greater buy-in and shared ownership of the results, which may also bring about further changes in perspectives and attitudes (Cousins, 2003).

For example, in a participatory evaluation, the evaluator trains participants, staff, and other stakeholders to gather and analyze data as evaluation partners and coevaluators. Active participants acquire inquiry skills, practice logical reasoning, and "are more likely to feel ownership not only of their findings but also of the inquiry process itself" (Patton, 2002, p. 184). Practitioners who take an active role in the evaluation can assist with data interpretation, clarify understanding, provide insights into the findings, and communicate any concerns regarding the process. Fully engaged practitioners often have a better understanding of the findings and ways to incorporate the results (O'Sullivan, 2004).

It is also important to note that involvement in the process should extend beyond rank-and-file project personnel. The project director or decision maker needs to take ownership of the evaluation process as well. This is important in nonformal settings given the lack of established infrastructure within which to convey the meaning of certain evaluation findings. From time to time, an overworked program administrator may feel a sense of relief that an external evaluator will take care of the evaluation portion of the grant requirement, giving the evaluator the sole responsibility to complete the evaluation. However, practitioners who take an active role in the evaluation can interpret data, clarify understanding, and provide insights into the findings—all activities that promote use.

**Implementation and Results.** Unlike formal education, nonformal education settings typically do not have shared understandings of assessment measures or longstanding demands for grades and progress reports that demonstrate the effectiveness of a program. Thus, to increase the utility of nonformal education evaluations, practitioners must provide explicit descriptions of the measures and their meanings. Improving evaluation use also requires greater creativity in disseminating the findings, given the looser nature of the organization (that is, sporadic meetings, seasonal staff, and more volunteer program participation). For example, a public library's reading program director may consider sending out a quarterly newsletter to all of its past, current, and prospective volunteers. The newsletter could feature one aspect of a recent evaluation, explaining who participated, what was measured, and how the findings might be implemented. Another way to increase instrumental use of evaluation in these settings is to assist with the implementation of some of the recommendations, bearing in mind that while the infrastructure to support recommended changes may be missing in nonformal settings, the bureaucracy and red tape may also be missing. Reexamining programs in light of the findings and asking staff to take action based on the recommendations may demonstrate the validity and importance of evaluation.

It is also critical to let program stakeholders know the results of the evaluation and elicit their suggestions for changes that might be implemented based on the results. Finally, using the lessons learned throughout the evaluation to inform future evaluation projects is a clear approach to increasing process use and one more way to maximize an evaluation investment.

As a final point, the unique staffing patterns and seasonal scheduling common among nonformal educational settings provide another opportunity for evaluation use during staff training and orientation, which presumably will happen more with increased staff turnover and the length of time between nonformal classes or sessions. Repeated references to the evaluation and dissemination of summary documents describing the evaluation may increase the potential conceptual applications of the evaluation information and enable a director to implement the evaluation results directly in training. Also, as in other settings, information about the evaluation should be shared through newsletters, press releases, and Web sites.

## Conclusion

The ultimate aim of a program evaluation is to use it, not merely to write a report that will sit on a shelf. Evaluators and practitioners must work together to see that the evaluation process is useful and influences change. We contend that decision makers in nonformal education programs can maximize the utility of their evaluation investment and improve program effectiveness by being more mindful of the potential uses for evaluation information. This chapter seeks to increase evaluation use by defining the different types of evaluation uses and offering some strategies to address the particular challenges of nonformal education settings (for example, fewer established measures of success, less-stable staff, and more pronounced dependence on external resources for support).

Given these differences, practitioners in nonformal education settings would benefit by acknowledging the need for an evaluator who is familiar with both the program and the nature of nonformal education and embraces participant involvement. In addition, the onus is on program directors to own the evaluation, disseminate the results in a variety of settings, and use results to inform decision making, which will encourage further conceptual use of the results. With these actions, evaluation can contribute to more effective nonformal education programs that will ultimately serve the public good.

## References

Alkin, M. C., and Taut, S. M. "Unbundling Evaluation Use." *Studies in Educational Evaluation*, 2003, *29*, 1–12.

Cousins, J. B. "Utilization Effects of Participatory Evaluation." In T. Kellaghan, D. Stufflebeam, and L. A. Wingate (eds.), *International Handbook of Educational Evaluation*. Norwell, Mass.: Kluwer, 2003.

Forss, K., Rebien, C. C., and Carlsson, J. "Process Use of Evaluations." *Evaluation*, 2002, *8*, 29–45.

Greene, J. G. "Stakeholder Participation and Utilization in Program Evaluation." *Evaluation Review,* 1988, *12*(2), 91–116.

Henry, G. T., and Mark, M. M. "Beyond Use: Understanding Evaluation's Influence on Attitudes and Actions." *American Journal of Evaluation,* 2003, *24*(3), 293–314.

Huie Hofstetter, C., and Alkin, M. C. "Evaluation Use Revisited." In T. Kellaghan and D. I. Stufflebeam (eds.), *International Handbook of Education Evaluation.* Norwell, Mass.: Kluwer, 2003.

Kirkhart, K. E. "Reconceptualizing Evaluation Use: An Integrated Theory of Influence." In V. J. Caracelli and H. Preskill (eds.), *The Expanding Scope of Evaluation Use.* New Directions for Evaluation, no. 88. San Francisco: Jossey-Bass, 2000.

Mark, M. M., and Henry, G. T. "The Mechanisms and Outcomes of Evaluation Influence." *Evaluation,* 2004, *10*(1), 40–57.

Mark, M. M., Henry, G. T., and Julnes, G. *Evaluation: An Integrated Framework for Understanding, Guiding, and Improving Policies and Programs.* San Francisco: Jossey-Bass, 2000.

O'Sullivan, R. G. *Practicing Evaluation: A Collaborative Approach.* Thousand Oaks, Calif.: Sage, 2004.

Patton, M. Q. *Utilization-Focused Evaluation: The New Century Text.* (3rd ed.) Thousand Oaks, Calif.: Sage, 1997.

Patton, M. Q. *Qualitative Research and Evaluation Methods.* (3rd ed.) Thousand Oaks, Calif.: Sage, 2002.

Rossi, P. H., Freeman, H. E., and Lipsey, M. W. *Evaluation: A Systematic Approach.* (6th ed.) Thousand Oaks, Calif.: Sage, 1999.

Taylor, E. W., and Caldarelli, M. "Teaching Beliefs of Non-Formal Environmental Educators: A Perspective from State and Local Parks in the United States." *Environmental Education Research,* 2004, *10*(4), 451–469.

Torres, R. T., and Preskill, H. "Evaluation and Organizational Learning: Past, Present, and Future." *American Journal of Evaluation,* 2001, *22*(3), 387–395.

Weiss, C. H., Murphey-Graham, E., and Birkeland, S. "An Alternate Route to Policy Influence: How Evaluations Affect D.A.R.E." *American Journal of Evaluation,* 2005, *26*(1), 12–30.

Zint, M., Kraemer, A., Northway, H., and Miyoun, L. "Evaluation of the Chesapeake Bay Foundation's Conservation Education Programs." *Conservation Biology,* 2002, *16*(3), 1–9.

KATE CLAVIJO *is an evaluation consultant working in Washington, D.C.*

M. LYNETTE FLEMING *operates a consulting business from Tucson, Arizona, that designs, facilitates, and evaluates environmental education programs and materials for educators.*

ELIZABETH F. HOERMANN *is an education specialist for the National Park Service working in the Northeast Center for Education Services, Lowell, Massachusetts.*

STACIE A. TOAL *is an evaluation studies doctoral student in the Department of Educational Policy and Administration at the University of Minnesota.*

KELLI JOHNSON *is an evaluation studies doctoral student in the Department of Educational Policy and Administration at the University of Minnesota.*

5

*This chapter recommends an educational role for evaluators in nonformal settings, including the development of program theory and long-term evaluation capacity building.*

# Evaluators as Educators: Articulating Program Theory and Building Evaluation Capacity

*Martha C. Monroe, M. Lynette Fleming, Ruth A. Bowman, Jeanne F. Zimmer, Tom Marcinkowski, Julia Washburn, Nora J. Mitchell*

The opportunity that evaluators have to be educators is well known. Patton (2002a, p. 93) emphatically states, "Every interaction with an evaluation client, participant, stakeholder, and user is a teaching opportunity." This chapter discusses two ways in which evaluators can help educate the staff of nonformal programs: helping them articulate the theory that drives their program and helping them build evaluation capacity within their organization.

## Articulating Program Theory

One challenge in working with nonformal educators is not that they lack understanding of the program's details but that they do not easily articulate why the dissected elements of the program achieve the program's goals.

**Nonformal Educators.** Although nonformal educators may lack specific education or evaluation training, they are generally knowledgeable about the content they teach and extremely passionate about the services they provide. This is evident in the way one naturalist described her work:

> As I remember my nature center days, I think the powerful thing was establishing a center and a program that was strongly connected to the community.

NEW DIRECTIONS FOR EVALUATION, no. 108, Winter 2005 © Wiley Periodicals, Inc.
Published online in Wiley InterScience (www.interscience.wiley.com) • DOI: 10.1002/ev.171

We were their source of all things environmental. We developed the county recycling center, we had award-winning school programs, we taught their teachers, and we had lists of public library books related to each of our program topics. They came to us for all kinds of information. It was our responsibility to provide the community with programs and opportunities to enhance their quality of life and protect the environment—for the future. Granted, we only served one midsized community, but at that scale, we could do it [Anonymous, personal communication, 2004].

There is no less passion among nonformal educators who work in historical or other types of settings:

Our program serves children and teachers in six county school systems. It provides rich opportunities to use the powerful stories and settings of Antietam and Monocacy National Battlefields to enhance classroom instruction. Learning experiences at the battlefields are powerful. They help make history lessons meaningful and personally relevant for students, encouraging them to explore and consider the causes, sacrifices, and lessons of the American Civil War and what those lessons mean for us today [Anonymous, personal communication, 2004].

Often nonformal educators are motivated not just by the benevolent and important mission of sharing knowledge and providing learning experiences for people, but by the deep desire to save the world with programs that benefit society through broader long-range goals such as increasing scientific literacy, promoting world peace, preventing global climate change, enhancing American democracy, preserving America's natural and cultural treasures, and eliminating homelessness. Although these are motivating, worthy goals, it is virtually impossible to evaluate whether a program will actually affect these types of changes. An evaluator's challenge is often to help program staff identify, evaluate, and assess short-term outcomes, as well as program logic, processes, and administration.

At the other extreme, perhaps because the long-range goals can be overwhelming, some nonformal educators are interested only in collecting participant satisfaction and feedback for program evaluation that is often too narrow and, on its own, has limited value for ongoing program improvement. One evaluator noted that when beginning to work with wildlife refuge and nature center staffs to determine what they would like to learn from evaluations, "I always hear—we just need to know that they liked it!" She went on to say:

I distinctly remember the school programs at a particular national wildlife refuge. Staff train teachers and chaperones and then they are out of the loop. The teachers come to the center, grab a knapsack, and conduct the program.

So staff really only want to find out that the teachers are happy and the kids learned something. But since they aren't interacting with the kids, they don't have much control over what is learned. They wanted to get posttests from every fourth grader (didn't know they could sample) with really simple general questions. For the pretest they were going to count hands when teachers asked the kids a question, "How many of you know the name of one animal that lives here?" [Anonymous, personal communication, 2004].

There is an array of other challenges an evaluator may encounter when beginning to work with nonformal education program staff. For example, some program staff want to accomplish a variety of learning outcomes in a program with limited contact time and want to assess participants over a broad range of those learning outcomes. One National Park Service education program that lasted two hours on-site with additional pre- and postvisit materials for classroom use was intended to teach about the Civil War, archeology, preservation of historic and cultural resources, local history, topography and mapping skills, and a variety of other learning outcomes. Working with evaluators helped staff refine the program design to be more realistic and then develop an approach to assessing participant outcomes commensurate with the amount of time and involvement they actually had with the program.

Evaluators in nonformal settings need to have a variety of evaluation methods and approaches to be responsive to the context. However, seldom do evaluators have the in-depth knowledge of the content area that the nonformal educators bring. So while the case has been made that nonformal educators generally have a lot to learn about evaluation, the same is generally true for the evaluators about the content and area of expertise that is the basis of the program. We suggest that successful evaluation activities are those in which the evaluator is an educator and through that role enables nonformal staff to share their knowledge and passion, identify reasonable evaluation goals, and gain a foundation in evaluation that will serve them through future program development opportunities.

**Nonformal Program Evaluation Tradition, History, and Practice.** It is often initially difficult for evaluators to engage program staff in helpful dialogue about evaluation goals because the staff may have never articulated the program's conceptual structure or compared the program's reality to the vision that motivates their work. The staff may believe ultimate goals are the only ones worth evaluating or think desired outcomes are too difficult to measure or attribute to their program. They may know some desired outcomes are not being reached but not why the program is failing to work as intended. Worse, they may not have thought about what their outcomes might be. The use of program theory and logic models is particularly important in these nonformal settings because the program may have developed out of an intuitive grasp of what is available and possible rather than a formal exploration of needs. This may be evident in the range of program outcomes discussed previously, including the extremes of idealism and the simple informality of documenting an enjoyable experience.

It is helpful for evaluators to understand these nearly ubiquitous challenges of nonformal program evaluation. Despite this difficulty, however, there are many opportunities for evaluators to assist nonformal program staff if they understand the multiple dimensions of this problem. It is more than a language barrier. To become helpful partners in the evaluation effort, staff members and stakeholders need to understand the fundamentals of program theory and the evaluation process, and evaluators need to be willing educators of program staff.

Program theory in evaluation is not in wide use in nonformal evaluation practice (Bickman, 1987). Most nonformal program evaluations have consisted of "black box" evaluations, which identify what goes into a program (inputs) and what comes out of a program (outputs), but without considering what goes on inside a program. For many staff in nonformal programs, "theory" simply means assertions about why the program should work (Bush, Mullis, and Mullis, 1995). An assessment of multiple studies reported in the *Journal of Extension* highlighted the prevalence of the "black box" method in nonformal program evaluation:

> One recent study reported on a teacher training program. The authors clearly defined problems to be addressed in this program, the objectives of the program, and how these objectives would be measured (Turner and Travnichek, 1992). Another study evaluating stress and coping programs reported its findings in much the same way (Fetsch, 1990). Both programs were reported as successful in meeting their objectives. What is not known is why they were successful. For example, what factors were leading contributors to making the program work? Was there a particular theory used as a basis for developing the program? If so, did the results support the theory? [Bush, Mullis, and Mullis, 1995]

The transition to theory-driven evaluations means an emphasis on the development and use of a more intricate framework that describes the basis of the program. When an evaluator joins the program after the program has been developed, it is sometimes necessary to recreate the program theory with nonformal program staff and stakeholders. That exercise, as explained below, is an educational one.

## Program Theory Approaches

When evaluators work with nonformal program stakeholders, it is first necessary to deconstruct and analyze the assumptions behind the program itself. This process can motivate program staff and illustrate the connections between the program's components. These program theory discussions can help the evaluator understand how and why programs work and what is accomplished as a result. Whether the evaluator chooses to speak of a logic model (W. K. Kellogg Foundation, 2004), a conceptual and action model (Chen, 1990), a program theory (Weiss, 1998), or the program's theory of action (Patton, 2002b), the nonformal partners need to understand what is meant.

The word *theory* refers to the practitioners' knowledge and intuition of what works, that is, their program theory. *Logic* refers to the logical connections among the program's invested resources (inputs) that allow activities to be accomplished (outputs) and the resulting benefits and changes (outcomes). Practitioners need to understand that the model is a helpful tool, but only a beginning step in evaluation, and that the model is not the evaluation plan, but a tool that helps decide what to evaluate and when. It provides conceptual understanding of complex programs and helps focus an evaluation. With the evaluator, staff can use a program theory model to clarify the evaluation's purpose, create evaluation questions, identify criteria, select data sources, establish key clients, and determine available resources.

For nearly forty years, evaluators have based program evaluation on causal models of programs (Rogers, Hacsi, Petrosino, and Huebner, 2000). There is a variety of terms, definitions, frameworks, and procedures for the kind of evaluation that is guided by an understanding of how a program causes intended or observed outcomes. Some of these variations that can be useful in nonformal program evaluation are highlighted here. Chen (1990) has described six types of theory-driven evaluation. Recently he added to his list a holistic assessment approach to program theory that includes prescriptive and descriptive assumptions underlying programs (Chen, 2004). Prescriptive assumptions, or change models, include a description of the actions that must be taken in a program so that change occurs. Descriptive assumptions, or action models, include descriptions of the causal processes that must occur to reach program goals. Huebner (2000) believes that by involving education staff in program theory development, the evaluation receives clarified program goals, cooperation and buy-in, and reflective practice.

Weiss (2003–2004) defines theory-based evaluation "as the logical series of steps that lays out the path from inputs to participant responses to further intervention to further participant responses and so on, until the goal is achieved (or breaks down along the way)" (p. 3). She posits three reasons that program theory has become popular for evaluation:

• It yields "a logical framework for planning data collection" (p. 3).
• It enables evaluators to monitor movement of the program and participants through a sequence of steps and claim causation even when randomized assignment is not possible.

- It contributes to the evaluator's understanding of how and why the program works.

Considering logic models, Patton (2002b) describes them as follows:

> A logic model or theory of action depicts, usually in graphic form, the connections between program inputs, activities and processes (implementation), outputs, immediate outcomes, and long-term impacts. . . . I distinguish a logic model from a theory of change. The only criterion for a logic model is that it be, well, *logical,* that is, that it portrays a reasonable, defensible, and sequential order from inputs through activities to outputs, outcomes, and impacts. A theory of change or theory of action, in contrast, bears the burden of specifying and explaining assumed, hypothesized, or tested causal links. Logic models are *descriptive.* Theory of change and theory of action models are *explanatory* and *predictive* [pp. 162–163].

The focus on program theory development includes the identification of both explicit and implicit objectives of program staff. Theories of action are explicit descriptions of how strategies and techniques produce outcomes. Theories of use are what is actually done in the field. A frequent challenge is that the two theories may be contradictory. The conceptualization of theories of action within programs derives from the work of Argyris and Schön (1974, 1978), who studied the connection between theory and practice as a means of increasing professional effectiveness within organizations:

> We begin with the proposition that people hold theories of action about how to produce consequences they intend. Such theories are theories about human effectiveness. By effectiveness we mean the degree to which people produce their intended consequences in ways that make it likely that they will continue to produce intended consequences. Theories of action, therefore, are theories about effectiveness, and because they contain propositions that are falsifiable, they are also theories about truth. Truth in this case means truth about how to behave effectively [Argyris, 1982, p. 83].
>
> Identifying both the theories-of-action and the theories-of-use is necessary in determining how a program works and helps bring together theory and practice [Kolb, 1992].

We believe these benefits of program theory are important for evaluators of nonformal programs to keep in mind. For evaluators who find themselves in a nonformal setting, we offer the following discussion of two program theory models. For nonformal educators who wish to evaluate a program, we encourage the use of the following discussion to take the first step in evaluation planning.

## Two Models for Nonformal Settings: Logic Models and Causal Mapping

Two models are particularly appropriate for nonformal settings because they help construct a better understanding of a program so that evaluation can occur. The first is the basic logic model (it is described in detail by the University of Wisconsin Extension at http://www.uwex.edu/ces/pdande/evaluation/evallogicmodel.html). The logic model uses the basic approach of identifying inputs, outputs, and outcomes. Work can start from either end, moving forward or backward (Taylor-Powell, 2002).

The second example is a form of causal mapping, as described in *Visible Thinking* (Bryson, Ackermann, Eden, and Finn, 2004). This methodology is particularly appropriate in nonformal settings because the process is straightforward, it uses common language, and it can be used to develop an action-oriented logic model. The process begins by asking simple questions:

1. What do you want to do?
2. How would you do that (or what would it take to do that)?
3. Why would you want to do that (or what would the consequences be of doing that)?

Rather than starting at the beginning or end, the *Visible Thinking* causal mapping approach, sometimes referred to as action-oriented strategy mapping or an action-oriented logic model, starts in the middle. While these questions might have been asked before the program was developed and answered with the program itself, an evaluator can begin the process of educating staff about program theory by using the same questions that recall the purpose and rationale of the program.

With either model, key needs for the evaluator and questions for the staff include the following:

*Identifying the goal.* What was the program designed to do? What problem are you solving with this program? Why do you offer these programs?
*Identifying a program theory.* Why do you think this program will solve that problem? How will your programs help achieve that goal? What about your program makes it possible to reach the goal? Is there any research that supports the links between the program and the goal?
*Revealing the less obvious connections.* What is it about your program that makes it effective?

The roles of the evaluator in the process of developing the program theory include those of constituent, another stakeholder, and consensus generator. The evaluator shares knowledge of evaluation and relevant information on similar programs, applicable policy, research, and theory (Chen, 1990). The evaluator educates.

**Essential Features of a Logic Model.** Using a logic model approach with nonformal educators can help them confront their expectations for the program. Evaluators can help nonformal educators understand the words used in the model in order to generate a useful evaluation plan. In the logic model, outputs and outcomes have specific meaning. The process involves identifying (see Figure 5.1):

- Inputs: What is invested?
- Outputs: What is done?
- Outcomes or Impacts: What are the results?

As staff and evaluators begin to work with the model and describe what is invested, what is done, and what results they expect to see, the logic model expands to include a description of the situation, assumptions, external factors, and priorities. The evaluator can help staff realize that the evaluation is only as good as the logical connections that form the arrows between the inputs, outputs, and outcomes. What evidence do they have to suggest that these short- and long-term changes are expected outcomes from these people engaging in those activities? How reasonable is this assumption? What else would have to be in place to see this type of change? What other variables might explain the same outcomes? Some of these factors can be identified as assumptions and external factors.

## Figure 5.1.  Logic Model Diagram

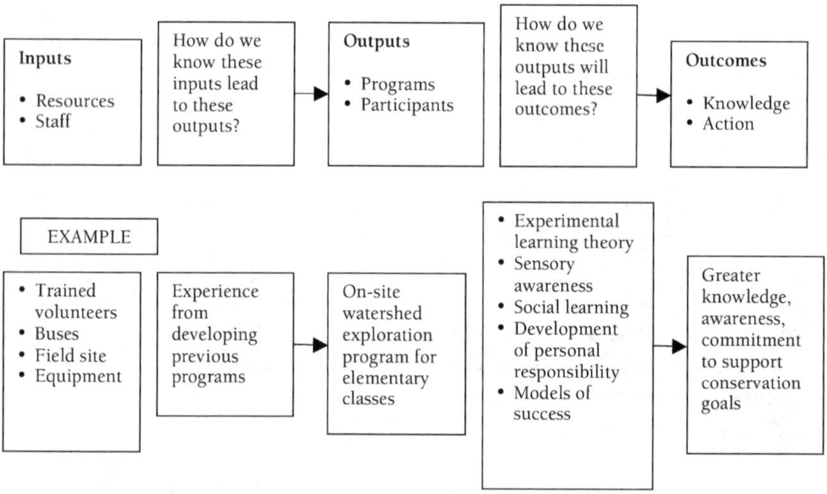

*Source:* This example is adapted from the University of Wisconsin website, which includes several graphics that may be useful in educating nonformal practitioners about program theory and logic models.

Evaluators need to help program staff realize that the further the outcomes are from the program outputs, the weaker is the influence of the program itself and the more likely it is that outside influences will affect measured results (Plantz, Greenway, and Hendricks, 1997). For this reason, many evaluations focus on outputs and shorter-term outcomes. If the logical links are reasonable and defensible, however, program staff should not mourn their inability to measure grandiose claims. Evaluators can help them understand that measuring the first tier of outcomes indicates the program is functioning as intended and could lead to ultimate outcomes. Unfortunately, few program theories in nonformal education are strong enough to promise convincingly that a program will save the world.

**Essential Features of Causal Mapping.** In nonformal settings, the program's implementation may not be clearly linked to its design. Furthermore, the reason for embarking on an evaluation may have multiple motivations (funding requirement, public relations, program improvement, and so on). Causal mapping is used to make sense of a program. The value to evaluation planning is that the process fleshes out criteria that are measurable and linked to the program goals. It may also reveal important meanings to the program staff that were not previously identified, and it has the potential to provide direction for improvement. As illustrated in Figure 5.2, causal mapping uses word and arrow diagrams to link ideas and actions,

**Figure 5.2. Causal Model Diagram**

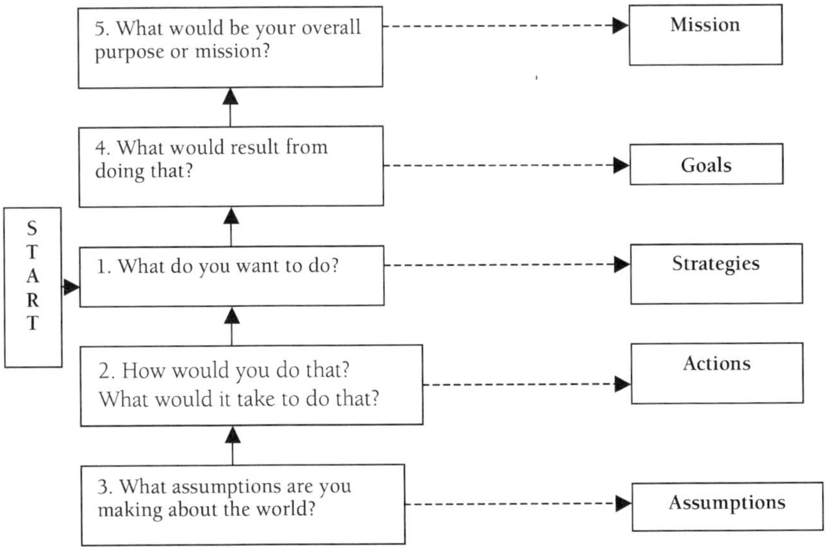

*Source:* Adapted from Bryson, Ackermann, Eden, and Finn (2004, p. 159).

which can help develop the program's theory of action. It is particularly conducive to engaging program staff and stakeholders.

Developing causal maps can require interaction on many levels. In order to make the mapping process one that can be enhanced over time and shared across locations, mapping software is available through several vendors. The Window-based Decision Explorer by Banxia is one such tool that has been used successfully with action-oriented strategy maps.

## Strategies to Build Capacity in Nonformal Education Organizations

Helping program staff articulate their program theory is one way evaluators can build evaluation capacity within nonformal education organizations. There are other ways evaluators can contribute to the evaluation skills of nonformal educators. Some nonformal educators are particularly interested in the opportunity to learn from the process of program evaluation. Indeed, they fully recognize the importance of evaluation and may also wish to build their professional portfolio to include evaluation skills.

Much can be done to enhance the culture of evaluation in the world of nonformal programs that will help prevent evaluation frustration and improve program quality. For example, in addition to clarifying initial assumptions about the program, evaluators can help nonformal programs make informed planning, implementation, and management decisions by addressing such questions as these:

- What should we expect from program activities?
- Who will benefit from the outputs?
- How can project activities be improved?
- How can we maximize the positive and minimize the negative outcomes?
- What do the program participants already know? What do they learn? What have they experienced? What are their ideas for program improvement?

**Identifying Primary Intended Users.** As they start planning the evaluation, staff could begin by identifying the stakeholders who will be the primary users of the evaluation, for without them, the effort involved in evaluation may be a poor use of resources. "As always the question of primary intended users is . . . primary" (Patton, 1997, p. 217). As defined by Patton, the primary intended users (PIUs) of the evaluation are those who are in a position to do or decide something regarding the program (a subset of all stakeholders). The first step in any evaluation process is usually to identify stakeholders, who may include those involved in program operations (administrators, staff, volunteers, contractors, sponsors, collaborators or coalition partners, funders), as well as those served or affected by the program (clients and participants, family members, neighborhood organizations, academic institutions, elected officials, advocacy groups, professional organizations, skeptics, opponents).

Although the identification of PIUs may be a simple process, understanding whether these staff actually have the ability to alter the program as a result of the evaluation may be less clear. In those cases, an assessment of the roles of the stakeholders will be useful in determining who and how they should be involved in the evaluation. The process of searching for the PIUs is one that an evaluator could facilitate with nonformal staff. In doing so, the evaluator is both educating and building the capacity of the staff to see their program in a new light.

It is unlikely that all nonformal education stakeholders will want or be able to be involved throughout the evaluation process, yet it is essential to the success of the evaluation process that the PIUs be identified and engaged. Patton emphasizes the importance of gathering information for specific individuals who will have the willingness, authority, and ability to put evaluation results to work. Without this focus on specific intended users, he argues, it is too easy to collect information that may be potentially interesting but will never be used. Engagement of PIUs is crucial in the determination of program theory, including the identification of validity assumptions where reduction of uncertainty about causal linkage is critical. Building the capacity of the PIUs may improve not only the use of the evaluation results but the quality of the evaluation itself.

**Building Evaluation Skills.**  There are common strategies that nonformal educators can undertake to increase their evaluation skills: professional development courses, mentoring, training, and the opportunity to participate in their own program evaluation. When evaluators work directly with nonformal educators in the development of these opportunities and in the role of educators, the increased communication and understanding may be beneficial to all.

Large organizations and agencies are more likely to have the resources to coordinate evaluation training. One such example is the U.S. Fish and Wildlife Service's course, Education Program Evaluation. In 1994 the U.S. Fish and Wildlife Service's National Conservation and Training Center began a process to increase the skills of program staff in evaluation. Two parallel needs assessments asked (1) staff what they knew about program evaluation and in what situations they would use it and (2) nonformal education and evaluation experts what ought to be presented in a short course (Monroe, 1995). That information, plus the experiences of the initial instructor team, formed the basis of a four-day course, Education Program Evaluation.

The course has been offered seven times, evolving slightly in each rendition to continue to meet the needs of participants while retaining the basic framework. It has also been adapted for distance education and is offered through the University of Wisconsin–Stevens Point. The purpose of the course is to provide participants with an overview of conducting evaluation for education and outreach programs and an opportunity to practice skills in designing and using evaluation tools. Emphasis is placed on formative evaluation that leads to improving program quality.

After an introduction to evaluation and the planning process, participants are introduced to several sites with nonformal programs or materials (usually a youth program, an exhibit area, an adult or family program, and a training workshop). During the course, they develop an evaluation plan and at least three data-collecting tools, administer those tools, analyze data, and present their findings to the group. The course participants share their results with the partnering organizations, which realize they are not getting a professional evaluation but are generally pleased to have any type of feedback about their programs.

This level of instruction, while extremely basic, is a necessary step to engage nonformal educators in evaluation. The four-day course introduces people to the process of thinking like a devil's advocate. An advanced course is needed to help nonformal educators develop the program theory links that will help them fill in the boxes between the arrows of the logic model.

Formal training opportunities are not the only way to build capacity. Mentoring, partnering, networking, and collaborating with colleagues are useful strategies to enable staff to see what others are doing and build a critical mass of nonformal educators learning from each other. In this sense, nonformal educators may have an advantage over formal educators. Although there is great diversity of programs across the nonformal community, the evaluation needs and questions are relatively similar. If staff can learn to look beyond the content differences to learn from evaluations at museums, libraries, parks, and airport kiosks, they will be able to increase their networking and learning opportunities. Evaluators could play a valuable role by linking interested educators.

When nonformal program leaders recognize the great need for capacity building among their staff and the equally great opportunity that exists to learn about evaluation through the process of doing one, they may wish to develop a contract for this process that includes both types of deliverables: program evaluation and training. The outcome of this effort will be not only an evaluation of the program but also program staff who are more aware of the value of evaluation, the process of evaluation, and the development of evaluation tools. Their increased capacity will help them develop new programs with an articulated program theory that will make future evaluations much easier. Consultants who can offer both services may see their workload increase as more administrators realize the importance of evaluation and the difficulty of building capacity on their own.

## Conclusion

Evaluators of nonformal education programs may be stymied by unintended outcomes, long-term impacts that defy clean measurement, and a myriad of other factors affecting the programs they evaluate. Evaluators often approach a project with a sense of what can be measured and documented and what cannot. Nonformal education staff can be taught to appreciate this distinction. Articulating program theories will help staff think more carefully about their program and the outcomes they can realistically and logically defend. For some, this is a milestone.

Tremendous potential exists to build an evaluation culture in the nonformal education community. Nonformal educators are coming to understand the advantages of integrating evaluation into all stages of program design and implementation. They know they need evaluative information to ensure continuous program improvement and optimize the use of limited funding and staff for maximum audience benefit. Nonformal education evaluators could embrace their dual roles of evaluator and capacity builder to help move the nonformal education community across the evaluation capacity continuum, working to institutionalize evaluation processes into the organizations they serve. If they do, all who participate in these important programs will be better served, and the long-term societal goals of nonformal education programs will have a better chance of saving the world, one bit at a time.

## References

Argyris, C. *Reasoning, Learning, and Action: Individual and Organizational.* San Francisco: Jossey-Bass, 1982.

Argyris, C., and Schön, D. *Theory in Practice: Increasing Professional Effectiveness.* San Francisco: Jossey-Bass, 1974.

Argyris, C., and Schön, D. *Organizational Learning: A Theory of Action Perspective.* Reading, Mass.: Addison-Wesley, 1978.

Bickman, L. (Ed.). *Using Program Theory in Evaluation.* New Directions for Program Evaluation, No. 33. San Francisco: Jossey-Bass, 1987.

Bryson, J., Ackermann, F., Eden, C., and Finn, C. B. *Visible Thinking: Unlocking Causal Mapping for Practical Business Results.* Hoboken, N.J.: Wiley, 2004.

Bush, C., Mullis, R., and Mullis, A. "Evaluation: An Afterthought or an Integral Part of Program Development?" *Journal of Extension,* 1995, 33(2). http://www.joe.org/joe/1995april/a4.html.

Chen, H. T. *Theory-Driven Evaluation.* Thousand Oaks, Calif.: Sage, 1990.

Chen, H. T. "The Roots of Theory-Driven Evaluation: Current Views and Origins." In M. Alkin (ed.), *Evaluation Roots: Tracing Theorists' Views and Influences.* Thousand Oaks, Calif.: Sage, 2004.

Fetsch, R. J. "Prevention Program Impacts." *Journal of Extension,* Spring 1990, pp. 34–35.

Huebner, T. A. "Theory-Based Evaluation: Gaining a Shared Understanding Between School Staff and Evaluators." In P. J. Rogers, T. A. Hacsi, A. Petrosino, and T. A.

Huebner (eds.), *Program Theory in Evaluation: Challenges and Opportunities.* New Directions in Evaluation, no. 87. San Francisco: Jossey-Bass, 2000.

Kolb, D. G. "The Practicality of Theory." *Journal of Experiential Education,* 1992, *15*(2), 24–27.

Monroe, M. C. "Needs and Preferences: Summary of Survey of Potential Participants in a FWS Program Evaluation Course." Unpublished report to the Division of Education and Outreach, National Conservation Training Center, U.S. Fish and Wildlife Service, Shepherdstown, W.Va., Sept. 7, 1995.

Patton, M. Q. *Utilization-Focused Evaluation: The New Century Text.* (3rd ed.) Thousand Oaks, Calif.: Sage, 1997.

Patton, M. Q. "Teaching and Training with Metaphors." *American Journal of Evaluation,* 2002a, *23*(1), 93–98.

Patton, M. Q. *Qualitative Research and Evaluation Methods.* (3rd ed.) Thousand Oaks, Calif.: Sage, 2002b.

Patton, M. Q. "Utilization-Focused Evaluation Checklist." 2002c. http://www.wmich. edu/evalctr/checklists/ufechecklist.htm.

Plantz, M. C., Greenway, M. T., and Hendricks, M. "Outcome Measurement: Showing Results in the Nonprofit Sector." In K. E. Newcomer (ed.), *Using Performance Measurement to Improve Public and Nonprofit Programs.* New Directions for Evaluation, no. 75. San Francisco: Jossey-Bass, 1997. http://www.unitedway.org/outcomes/ndpa-per.html.

Rogers, P. J., Hacsi, T. A., Petrosino, A., and Huebner, T. A. "Program Theory Evaluation: Practice, Promise, and Problems." In P. J. Rogers, T. A. Hacsi, A. Petrosino, and T. A. Huebner (eds.), *Program Theory in Evaluation: Challenges and Opportunities.* New Directions in Evaluation, no. 87. San Francisco: Jossey-Bass, 2000.

Taylor-Powell, E. "Program Development and Evaluation: Logic Model." University of Wisconsin-Extension, Madison, 2002. http://www.uwex.edu/ces/pdande/evaluation/evallogicmodel.htm.

Turner, J., and Travnichek, R. J. "Measuring the Success of Teacher Training." *Journal of Extension,* Winter 1992, *30*, 38.

Weiss, C. H. *Evaluation: Methods for Studying Programs and Policies.* (2nd ed.) Upper Saddle River, N.J.: Prentice Hall, 1998.

Weiss, C. H. "On Theory-Based Evaluation: Winning Friends and Influencing People." *Evaluation Exchange,* 2003–2004, *9*(4). http://www.gse.harvard.edu/hfrp/eval/issue24/theory.html.

W. K. Kellogg Foundation. *Logic Model Development Guide.* Battle Creek, Mich.: W. K. Kellogg Foundation, 2004.

MARTHA C. MONROE *is associate professor and extension specialist in the School of Forest Resources and Conservation at the University of Florida.*

M. LYNETTE FLEMING *operates an evaluation consulting business from Tucson, Arizona.*

RUTH A. BOWMAN *is an evaluation studies doctoral student in the Department of Educational Policy and Administration at the University of Minnesota.*

JEANNE F. ZIMMER *is an evaluation studies doctoral student in the Department of Educational Policy and Administration at the University of Minnesota.*

TOM MARCINKOWSKI is professor of education in the Science and Mathematics Education Department at the Florida Institute of Technology.

JULIA WASHBURN is vice president for grants and programs at the National Park Foundation, the congressionally chartered nonprofit partner of the National Park Service.

NORA J. MITCHELL is director of the National Park Service's Conservation Study Institute in Woodstock, Vermont.

*This chapter discusses four creative methods for addressing the special methodological challenges of nonformal education programs.*

# Creative Data Collection in Nonformal Settings

*Laurene Christensen, Julie E. Nielsen, Christopher M. Rogers, Boris Volkov*

This chapter examines some of the challenges to data collection in evaluating nonformal education programs and suggests creative methods for addressing those challenges. To begin, we remind the reader that some of the differences between formal and nonformal education can be summarized with the following definitions:

> *Formal education:* the hierarchically structured, chronologically graded "education system," running from primary school through the university and including, in addition to general academic studies, a variety of specialized programs and institutions for full-time technical and professional training.

> *Nonformal education:* any organized educational activity outside the established formal system—whether operating separately or as an important feature of some broader activity—that is intended to serve identifiable learning clienteles and learning objectives [Smith, 2005].

Evaluation is important in both formal and nonformal settings, and various pressures constrain any evaluation. Mertens (2005) identifies a number of typical constraints that influence evaluation decisions, including money, time, personnel, other existing contextual constraints, and politics. Patton (1997) states that understanding the intended use for an evaluation by intended users is imperative to making methods decisions. He acknowledges

that limitations in time and resources necessitate trade-offs, that "no design is perfect" (p. 243), and that there are no universal criteria for judging the quality of various methods. He emphasizes that it is important to discuss methods and make decisions before data collection begins in order to avoid later conflict.

## Challenges to Data Collection in Evaluating Nonformal Education Programs

Certain challenges are inherent in collecting data to evaluate nonformal education programs and settings. One challenge relates to the complexity of the educational system in which nonformal learning takes place. Separating the learning effects of a nonformal education program on participants from the effects of other essential elements of their daily learning process (for example, school experiences, students' background, family environment, and participation in other nonformal programs) may be a daunting task. With so many interacting factors, Thompson and others (2000) suggest that conventional experimental designs may not produce adequate information to determine what factors are producing particular outcomes.

Other challenges are associated with the drop-in nature of nonformal education, the range of variables that can define program quality, the multiple goals associated with these programs, and the fact that participants may involve themselves in several programs targeting the same learning need. In the next sections, we expand on these challenges to data collection in evaluating nonformal education programs.

**Drop-In Programs.**  Given the drop-in nature of some nonformal education programs (for example, see Volkov and King, 2003), it may be difficult for programs to encourage a large number of learners to participate consistently and ensure meaningful learning interactions with them. Since many participants do not attend on a regular basis, different participants are likely to receive different "doses" of the educational treatment. Contributing to the difficulty of evaluating drop-in programs is the fact that program staff may not have the capacity or the systems to track participation or even to maintain accurate databases with contact information. As a result, ongoing evaluation input from participants may be unavailable, necessitating full data collection with each learning episode.

**Wide Range of Variables.**  Another challenge of collecting data on nonformal settings is the range of variables that can define program quality. In their discussion of out-of-school program quality features, Yohalem, Pittman, and Wilson-Ahlstrom (2004) indicate that a program can show the presence or the lack of the following:

Youth opportunities
• Positive relationships
• Safety and belonging

- Exploration and skill building
- Meaningful involvement
- Expression and reflection

Staff practices that promote
- Youth as partners
- Safe, fair environments
- Supportive relationships
- Personalized participation
- Learning opportunities and intentional skill building
- Continuity within program and across settings

These elements of quality programming do not lend themselves to simple evaluation designs. It may be necessary to combine these indicators with other assessment constructs for implementing, evaluating, and fine-tuning a continuous improvement system in nonformal education. Indeed, taking all of these features into account when evaluating a nonformal education program requires the use of a wide variety of data collection methods.

**Multiple Goals.** Nonformal education programs often have multiple goals, and participants may come to the programs with additional goals in mind. For example, senior citizens attending a computer literacy course may be intending not only to learn how to use the Internet but also to seek a social outlet. In such cases, surveys may not address all of the program's goals, and tests of knowledge may not measure the most important outcomes of the program. Furthermore, there may be additional unintended outcomes unique to each participant that are difficult to measure.

**Participant Involvement in Multiple Nonformal Education Programs.** Evaluation of these programs may be further constrained due to participants' involvement in multiple programs. When nonformal education is delivered through multiple sources, how can an evaluator know the extent of the target program's success? For example, Hill (2005) found that prostitutes learned about HIV/AIDS prevention from a range of programs: doctors' offices, street outreach workers, music videos, Internet Web sites, and other prostitutes. The cumulative effect of all of these efforts may be more significant than any one program alone, so measuring the individual effect of one nonformal education program can be challenging. The fact that both nonformal programs and their participants can differ in the breadth, depth, intensity, duration, and intended goals for the learning experience limits the evaluation design and data collection choices for evaluations. These challenges, however, are not insurmountable. With creativity and persistence, evaluators can find appropriate data collection approaches to help nonformal educators improve the programs they deliver. In the next section, we highlight a few creative examples.

## Examples of Creative Data Collection Approaches

The following examples illustrate how evaluators faced with atypical audiences, settings, or programs can gather meaningful information for use in formative and summative evaluations.

**Kiddie Focus Groups.** Wells developed "kiddie focus groups" to help design a nature center to serve children (M. Wells, personal communication, September 13, 2005). As a formative evaluation, Wells took children on field trips to a variety of nature centers, parks, and zoos. The children were given surveys to evaluate how interesting they found each site. After visiting several sites, the children came together with Wells to discuss what was good, bad, and otherwise about those sites. The children gave their ideas on the development of the new site, and ultimately a set of interpretive principles was developed to guide the design of the new site. This evaluator successfully adapted the focus group strategy to her audience by making questions simple and explaining the purpose and intent of the evaluation to the children. The use of kiddie focus groups addressed the challenge of multiple goals in nonformal education programs by obtaining input directly from those affected by the program to target the most valued goals. Similarly, kiddie focus groups could be framed around predetermined indicators of quality. For example, using the qualities described previously, the facilitator could ask participants about the program's effect on positive relationships, safety and belonging, exploration and skill building, meaningful involvement, and expression and reflection.

**Naive Notions.** Borun (1990) of the Franklin Institute Science Museum in Philadelphia developed a technique called Naive Notions. In the context of her work in museum settings, Borun recognized that visitors often had misperceptions about gravity and that they were bringing these perceptions to their understanding of exhibits on gravity. She wanted to uncover people's naive notions and develop exhibits that would resolve these misunderstandings. To do so, she conducted front-end interviews to determine preexisting notions about gravity, designed a series of mock-up exhibits, interviewed visitors following their viewing of the mock-ups, and modified the exhibits on the basis of these results. Follow-up interviews demonstrated that visitors' misconceptions surrounding gravity decreased significantly.

The Naive Notions process may be useful to nonformal educators in programs with multiple goals to compare their existing conceptions regarding what the program should do against an array of possibilities. This clarifying exercise should enable the evaluation to focus on the most important goals.

**Archival Data.** A third example is provided by Wells and Butler (2004), who used archival data, including guest books, gift shop purchases linked to postal codes, and donation boxes as unobtrusive means for collecting data.

These records are often created for other purposes but can provide a wealth of information to evaluators. For example, by examining the postal codes of people making gift shop purchases, the evaluator can often determine where visitors live and can analyze purchasers in the context of a variety of demographic indicators, including income level, educational attainment, and proportion of rental properties versus owner-occupied units. A spatial analysis using the postal codes can inform program staff whether they are reaching their target audiences, the extent to which certain demographic groups are either over- or underrepresented, and so forth. The use of archival data may address challenges inherent in drop-in programs, by providing baseline and demographic data.

**Post-it® Surveys.**  Judy Machen (n.d.) of the Bradbury Museum in Los Alamos, New Mexico, developed a technique called Post-it® Surveys. She initially designed this data collection method to evaluate participants' understanding of the scientific content of an exhibit. Machen placed a large easel in the museum lobby. At the top of the white paper was a question about the exhibit's content. Located near the easel were pens and sticky notes for participants to use to respond to the evaluation question. Machen found that participants were very interested in using the sticky notes to respond to the question, and soon participants also began to respond to each other's sticky notes as well. Machen was able to compile the information from her surveys to bring back to the scientists and designers of the exhibit. They then redesigned the exhibit according to the participants' feedback.

The use of sticky note surveys can address challenges associated with the drop-in nature of nonformal education programs, programs with multiple goals, and programs that serve individuals participating in multiple programs to meet similar learning needs. For example, by having the sticky note surveys available at all times, nonformal educators can collect data from a number of participants at any time, even those who participate sporadically or only once. In addition, to address the challenge of multiple goals, questions can ask participants to write statements that reflect their top three learning goals and whether these goals were met. To address the challenge of individuals who access several programs for similar learning goals, questions could ask how this particular program differs from other nonformal education programs they attend. The convenience of the survey board allows collecting data on a wide range of carefully worded questions to inform decision making about ideas, content, presentation, and so on (Wells and Butler, 2004).

**The Talk Aloud.**  Another creative approach to data collection is a talk aloud. Similar to think-aloud evaluations done for usability testing, talk alouds ask participants to say what they see or what they are thinking as they encounter an exhibit or experience a component of a nonformal education program. M. Wells (personal communication, September 13, 2005) has used talk alouds with museum participants, and she suggests that this technique can be used for both formative and summative evaluations. A participant walks through an exhibit with an evaluator, who asks the participant to talk aloud about what he is seeing as well as what reactions he has as he makes sense of the exhibit. This technique elicits participants' subjective views of the exhibits that yield good insights, especially helpful at the formative stage of the evaluation. It can be particularly useful for programs that are pursuing multiple goals and those with a range of variables to define quality. By guiding the talk aloud, for example, the evaluator can prompt the participant to talk about the goals that the nonformal education program is seeking to address or to discuss the agreed-on quality variables. The interactive nature of the talk aloud provides opportunities to observe initial subjective reactions as well as to encourage the responder to elaborate for deeper understanding.

Table 6.1 summarizes the four data collection challenges we have presented in this chapter and the examples addressing each one.

## Conclusion

In this chapter we have identified a number of data collection challenges that may have an impact on design and methods in evaluating nonformal education programs. It is clear that evaluators are approaching nonformal education evaluation with creative data collection strategies that have the ability to address these challenges, provide reliable information, and assist program delivery staff in improving their education programs. This discussion can serve as a springboard for considering other creative approaches to the challenges of data collection in evaluating nonformal evaluation programs.

### Table 6.1.  Data Collection Examples

| Data Collection Challenge | Creative Approach |
|---|---|
| Drop-in nature of the program | Post-it® Survey<br>Archival Data |
| Range of variables that can define program quality | Talk Aloud<br>Kiddie Focus Groups |
| Multiple goals associated with nonformal education | Talk Aloud<br>Post-it® Survey<br>Naive Notions<br>Kiddie Focus Groups |
| Participant involvement in multiple nonformal education programs targeting the same learning need | Post-it® Survey |

## References

Borun, M. "Naive Notions and the Design of Science Museum Exhibits." In A.o.S.-T. Centers (ed.), *What Research Says About Learning in Science Museums.* Washington, D.C.: Association of Science-Technology Centers, 1990.

Hill, R. J. "Poz-itively Transformational: Sex Workers and HIV/AIDS Education." In J. Egan (ed.), *HIV/AIDs Education for Adults.* New Directions for Adult and Continuing Education, no. 105. San Francisco: Jossey-Bass, 2005.

Machen, J. (n.d.). "The Writing on the Wall." Unpublished technical document. Los Alamos, N.M.: Bradbury Science Museum.

Mertens, D. M. *Research and Evaluation in Education and Psychology: Integrating Diversity with Quantitative, Qualitative, and Mixed Methods.* Thousand Oaks, Calif.: Sage, 2005.

Patton, M. Q. *Utilization Focused Evaluation: The New Century Text.* (3rd ed.) Thousand Oaks, Calif.: Sage, 1997.

Smith, M. K. (ed.). *The Encyclopedia of Informal Education.* 2005. http://www.infed.org/biblio/b-nonfor.htm.

Thompson, A., and others. "Iowa Consortium for Assessment of Learning with Technology: A Collaborative Project." Paper presented at the International Conference on Learning Technology, Philadelphia, March, 2000. http://l2l.org/iclt/2000/papers/207a.pdf.

Volkov, B., and King, J. A. "Report of STUDIO 3D Project Evaluation." 2003. http://www.smm.org/studio3d/Studio%203D%20Eval%20Report.pdf.

Wells, M., and Butler, B. "Helpful Hints for Understanding the Effects of Botanical Garden Programs." *Public Garden,* 2004, *19*(92), 11–12. http://www.aabga.org/public_html/resrcs/tpg19–2.pdf.

Yohalem, N., Pittman, K., and Wilson-Ahlstrom, A. "Getting Inside the 'Black Box' to Measure Program Quality." *Evaluation Exchange,* 2004, *10*(1), 6–7.

LAURENE CHRISTENSEN *is a doctoral student in comparative and international development education in the Department of Educational Policy and Administration at the University of Minnesota.*

JULIE E. NIELSEN *is an evaluation studies doctoral student in the Department of Educational Policy and Administration at the University of Minnesota.*

CHRISTOPHER M. ROGERS *is a doctoral student in comparative and international development education in the Department of Educational Policy and Administration at the University of Minnesota.*

BORIS VOLKOV *is an evaluation studies doctoral student in the Department of Educational Policy and Administration at the University of Minnesota.*

*7*

*This chapter offers insights related to the value of involving evaluation early in the program development process and helping funders understand the benefits of evaluation.*

# Another Perspective: An Interview with David Smith

*Ruth A. Bowman, Kelli Johnson*

To provide another perspective on evaluation within nonformal settings, *New Directions for Evaluation* recently interviewed David Smith, the coordinator of the Professional Learning to Close the Achievement Gap program for the Kansas City, Kansas, Public Schools, who has extensive background in education and educational research. He formerly held positions with the Partnership for Children (a child advocacy organization), the Annenberg Institute for School Reform, and the Kettering Foundation. We asked him to reflect on his experiences with evaluating these programs from the perspective of program staff, evaluator, and funder.

NEW DIRECTIONS: What are the critical aspects of nonformal education that influence the evaluation of these programs?

DAVID SMITH: Everything matters, but one aspect that gets less attention than it should is building the knowledge base among nonformal education practitioners about the field of evaluation. Frequently, programs seek evaluation services only after programs are up and running—in a manner akin to designing the brakes while the car is speeding down the highway.

I worked for a program that supported the creation of after-school programs for middle school students. They obtained funding to begin the program, but before they could expand, they needed to quickly demonstrate

impressive program impact. So they brought in evaluators at that point rather than at the beginning, during the program design phase.

In addition, many nonformal programs feel pressure to use evaluation to "prove" something to individuals outside the field. In youth development work, for example, many evaluators recognize that the important outcomes are whether the youth achieve the developmental milestones toward becoming well-functioning, productive adults. We know that access to supports and opportunities (for example, high-quality after-school programs) makes them more likely to reach these milestones.

Unfortunately, many policymakers are focused on how many acts of violence were prevented or how much grades and test scores improved. Especially in times of scarce funding, this situation results in many well-meaning program directors' promising things that evaluation really can't deliver.

NEW DIRECTIONS: What advice do you have for novices or other evaluators new to nonformal settings? What is the most important characteristic for an evaluator of a nonformal program?

DAVID SMITH: Evaluators who find themselves in unfamiliar nonformal education settings should be sure to learn about the field they are working in rather than counting on the local program to have that knowledge. Such evaluators will also be well served by getting in on the ground floor of planning the program design rather than being brought in after the program is up and running. Evaluators who are conversant about the state of research and evaluation in that field and bring new information to the table will have substantially more credibility and voice at the table.

NEW DIRECTIONS: What specific evaluation practices have been particularly effective in working with nonformal programs and settings?

DAVID SMITH: It is particularly effective for evaluators to build relationships with the program funders by educating them about best practices in both the program area and the evaluation of that area. Educated funders can be extremely helpful in ensuring that a thoughtful evaluation component is built into the program design. If funders have a deep understanding of evaluation and what it can tell them about the work they are being asked to fund, they will be better able and much more likely to build resources into their grant making to support quality evaluations.

NEW DIRECTIONS: Describe the best practices in data collection for evaluation of nonformal programs. What methods work well?

NEW DIRECTIONS FOR EVALUATION • DOI 10.1002/ev

DAVID SMITH: First, the methods for evaluating nonformal education programs and settings are very program and field specific. Next, the best evaluations employ a strong degree of standardization in data collection, and they provide training *before* the program starts. Finally, the top programs also provide funding for data collection as a part of the grants.

NEW DIRECTIONS: Why is this volume of *New Directions* needed?

DAVID SMITH: I think this is a critical area of evaluation growth, in part because of what we are learning about the important role that nonformal education programs play in youth development—information that has come from the field of evaluation.

NEW DIRECTIONS: What should be next in the evolution of evaluation in nonformal settings?

DAVID SMITH: As I mentioned earlier, it is critically important for evaluators to build relationships with the program funders. This can be done by taking the time to educate funders about program and evaluation best practices in a particular issue area. Funders who understand the important contributions evaluation offers a program are more likely to support resources for evaluation as part of their grant-making process.

*RUTH A. BOWMAN is an evaluation studies doctoral student in the Department of Educational Policy and Administration at the University of Minnesota.*

*KELLI JOHNSON is an evaluation studies doctoral student in the Department of Educational Policy and Administration at the University of Minnesota.*

NEW DIRECTIONS FOR EVALUATION • DOI 10.1002/ev

# INDEX

Ackermann, F., 63, 69
Ahmed, M., 7, 12
Alkin, M. C., 48, 49, 54, 55
Argyris, C., 62, 69
Authors' retreat, 1–2, 11

Beck, L., 18
Bennett, C., 34, 42, 45
Bentrup, G., 29, 45
Bickman, L., 60, 69
Birkeland, S., 49, 55
Blahna, D., 29, 45
Boards, advisory and director, 10, 34–37
Borun, M., 76, 79
Bottom-up education, 7
Bowman, R. A., 3, 57, 70, 81, 83
Bradbury Museum, Los Alamos, New Mexico, 77
Brown, R. D., 23, 26, 27
Bryson, J., 63, 69
Burke, B., 30, 42, 45
Bush, C., 50, 69
Butler, B., 76, 79

Cable, T. T., 18
Caldarelli, M., 50, 55
Carlsson, J., 49, 54
Causal mapping, 63, 64–66
Chavez, D., 29, 46
Chen, H. T., 61, 64, 69
Chenery, L., 8, 11
Chesapeake Bay Foundation, Maryland, 48
Childress, R., 8, 11
Christensen, L., 3, 73, 79
Civitarese, S., 8, 12
Clavijo, K., 2, 47, 55
Colorado Department of Education, 35
Colorado Division of Wildlife, 31, 32, 33, 35, 41, 42
Committee on Audience Research and Evaluation, 30, 45
Constructivist learning model, 52
Coombs, P. H., 7, 12
Corporation for Public Broadcasting, 7, 12
Cousins, J. B., 32, 43, 45, 52, 54
Cronbach, C. J., 17, 27

D'Agostino, A., 32, 46
Data collection, 9, 15, 16, 30, 36, 37–39, 41, 44, 49, 61, 67, 68, 73–79, 82–83
Denver Zoological Foundation, 31, 32, 33, 34, 35, 41, 42, 45
Diamond, J., 30, 45
Disinger, J., 8, 12
Donaldson, S. I., 37, 45

Earl, L. M., 43
Eden, C., 63, 69
Educators, nonformal: characteristics of, 57–59; integration of evaluation into programs by, 69
Elasticity, 9
*Encyclopedia of Nonformal Education* (Smith, M. K.), 7
Environmental education, 1, 7, 21, 42; examples, 15, 52, 53; field experience in, 48; frequency of high-quality evaluation of, 43; guidelines for nonformal, 17, 30; program characteristics, 7–8; stakeholders, 29–45
Etling, A., 7, 8, 12
Evaluability assessment, 16, 33–34, 40–41
Evaluation: benefits of, 40–43; best practices, 82–83; "black box," 60; capacity building, 2, 5, 42, 43, 44, 57, 66–68; characterization of, historically, 13; collaborative, 32, 44; constraints, 73; culture of, enhancing, 66, 69; formative, 52, 68, 76, 77; funding, 33, 40, 83; inclusive approaches to, 43; influence, 47–48; methodological challenges of, 3, 15, 21, 26, 59, 60, 73–79; observations about, 50–51; participatory approaches to, 19, 30, 32, 43–44, 52–53; plan components, 37; plan development, 34–37; primary intended users (PIUs) of, 66–67; reasons for, 65; reflective, 26; situational, 25; theory-driven, 60, 61; universal issues of, 5; use, 2, 5, 19, 24, 33, 41–44, 47–54
Evaluators: as educators, 17, 26, 57, 60, 64, 67; and evaluands, shared values of, 2, 14, 21; key need for, and questions for staff, 63, 66; most important

85

# Back Issue/Subscription Order Form

Copy or detach and send to:

**Jossey-Bass, A Wiley Imprint, 989 Market Street, San Francisco CA 94103-1741**

**Call or fax toll-free: Phone 888-378-2537 6:30AM – 3PM PST; Fax 888-481-2665**

Back Issues:     Please send me the following issues at $27 each
(Important: please include series initials and issue number, such as EV101.)

_____

_____

_____

$ _____     Total for single issues

$ _____     SHIPPING CHARGES: SURFACE    Domestic      Canadian

| | Domestic | Canadian |
|---|---|---|
| First Item | $5.00 | $6.00 |
| Each Add'l Item | $3.00 | $1.50 |

For next-day and second-day delivery rates, call the number listed above.

Subscriptions:    Please __start __renew my subscription to *New Directions Evaluation* for the year 2 _____ at the following rate:

| | | |
|---|---|---|
| U.S. | __Individual $80 | __Institutional $185 |
| Canada | __Individual $80 | __Institutional $225 |
| All Others | __Individual $104 | __Institutional $259 |

**For more information about online subscriptions visit
www.interscience.wiley.com**

$ _____    Total single issues and subscriptions (Add appropriate sales tax for your state for single issue orders. No sales tax for U.S. subscriptions. Canadian residents, add GST for subscriptions and single issues.)

__Payment enclosed (U.S. check or money order only)

__VISA __MC __AmEx #_____ Exp. Date _____

Signature _____ Day Phone _____

__ Bill Me (U.S. institutional orders only. Purchase order required.)

Purchase order # _____

Federal Tax ID13559302           GST 89102 8052

Name _____

Address _____

_____

Phone _____ E-mail _____

For more information about Jossey-Bass, visit our Web site at www.josseybass.com

OTHER TITLES AVAILABLE IN THE
NEW DIRECTIONS FOR EVALUATION SERIES
Jean A. King, Editor-in-Chief